The
New
Testament
Canon

The New Testament Canon

Its Making and Meaning

by

Harry Y. Gamble

Wipf and Stock Publishers
EUGENE, OREGON

Wipf and Stock Publishers
150 West Broadway
Eugene, Oregon 97401

The New Testament Canon
Its Making and Meaning
By Gamble, Harry Y.
Copyright©1985 Augsburg Fortress Publishing
ISBN: 1-57910-909-8
Publication Date: March, 2002
Previously published by Fortress Press, 1985.

Contents

5

Editor's Foreword

The volumes in this series have dealt with issues of method and of form. They have described and analyzed various critical procedures for understanding NT texts (form and redaction criticism, literary criticism, structural exegesis, etc.). They also have attempted to define a number of the formal patterns which shape the materials of the New Testament (gospel, letter, proverb, apocalypse, etc.). The volume on NT theology was not a departure from this direction because it dealt with such formal questions as the definition of NT theology, the motives which have generated its pursuit, and its relationship to other theological disciplines. The focus of the series has been on the formal and the critical, with attention to both the linguistic-literary and the historical paradigms for the critical study of the NT, as well as to the dimension of meaning.

The present volume on the canon continues this tradition. It is a historical analysis of a fundamentally theological phenomenon. Professor Gamble deals historically with the development of the canon and the factors which generated its formation. But this development was composed of confessional decisions. The variety of forms in the NT, which can be interpreted with a multiplicity of methods, became a closed collection which a believing community regarded as religiously authoritative. Thus, as Professor Gamble well demonstrates, a historical study of the canon's formation cannot be truly critical without paying due attention to the theological factors in the historical process and the theological implications of the church's decision to have a canon. It is necessary to deal with such issues as the context which the canon provides for interpretation and the question of how the canon can exercise normative authority for Christianity.

DAN O. VIA

The Divinity School
Duke University

Abbreviations

Adv. Marc.	Tertullian, *Adversus Marcionem* [*Against Marcion*]
A.H.	Irenaeus, *Adversus haereses* [*Against Heresies*]
Apol.	Justin, *Apology*
ATR	*Anglican Theological Review*
BA	*Biblical Archaeologist*
B.C.E.	Before the Common Era
BHT	Beiträge zur historischen Theologie
Bib	*Biblica*
BJRL	Bulletin of the John Rylands University Library of Manchester
CBQ	*Catholic Biblical Quarterly*
C.E.	Common Era
CTM	Concordia Theological Monthly
Dial.	Justin, *Dialogus cum Trypho* [*Dialogue with Trypho*]
Ep.	*Epistle(s)*
EvTh	*Evangelische Theologie*
fl.	floruit [flourished]
H.E.	Eusebius, *Historia ecclesiastica* [*Ecclesiastical History*]
HBT	*Horizons in Biblical Theology*
HeyJ	*Heythrop Journal*
HTR	*Harvard Theological Review*
HTS	Harvard Theological Studies
IDBSup.	*Interpreter's Dictionary of the Bible* supplementary volume
Int	*Interpretation*
JBC	*The Jerome* Bible
JBL	*Journal of Biblical Literature*
JTS	*Journal of Theological Studies*
JSOT	*Journal for the Study of the Old Testament*

KBANT	Kommentare und Beiträge zum Alten und Neuen Testament
ms(s).	manuscript(s)
MThZ	*Münchener theologische Zeitschrift*
NT	New Testament
NTS	*New Testament Studies*
NovTSup	Novum Testamentum, Supplement
OT	Old Testament
RBen	*Revue bénédictine*
RHPR	*Revue d'histoire et de philosophie religieuses*
SBLMS	Society of Biblical Literature, Monograph Series
SBS	Stuttgarter Bibelstudien
SBT	Studies in Biblical Theology
SD	Studies and Documents
SPAW.PH	Sitzungsberichte der preussischen Akademie der Wissenschaften—Philosophisch-historische Klasse
StEv	*Studia evangelica*
StPat	*Studia patristica*
StTh	*Studia theologica*
Strom.	Clement of Alexandria, *Stromateis*
TDNT	*Theological Dictionary of the New Testament*
TS	*Theological Studies*
TU	Texte und Untersuchungen
VC	*Vigiliae christianae*
WMANT	Wissenschaftliche Monographien zum Alten und Neuen Testament
WUNT	Wissenschaftliche Untersuchungen zum Neuen Testament
ZKG	*Zeitschrift für Kirchengeschichte*
ZNW	*Zeitschrift für die neutestamentlische Wissenschaft*
ZTK	*Zeitschrift für Theologie und Kirche*

I

Introduction

THE PROBLEM OF
THE NEW TESTAMENT CANON

Even a cursory glance at its contents reveals that what we know as "the New Testament" is not a book at all in the usual sense but a collection of early Christian writings, twenty-seven in all. It is a collection, moreover, which has historically been set apart as possessing a distinctive and indeed unique authority for the faith and practice of the Christian church. As a fixed collection of religiously authoritative literature, the NT constitutes the *canon* of Christian scriptures.[1] The purpose of this volume is to assess the NT as canon and thus to comprehend the fundamental form of the NT itself. NT scholarship has been progressively sensitive to the importance of form as a component—along with content—of meaning, and the NT has been greatly illuminated through the formal analysis of the traditions and documents contained in it. But all too little attention has been paid to the form of the NT *as a whole*, although an understanding of that form is indispensable to a full appreciation of the meaning and function of the NT. An evaluation of the NT as canon entails historical, literary, and theological questions: How did this collection of writings come into being? What assumptions and intentions contributed to its formation? Who or what determined its contents? On what basis did special authority come to be attached to these writings? How does the character of this collection bear upon its interpretation? In what ways does this collection claim or exercise religious authority?

Such questions are rarely raised by the ordinary reader, even the

1. On the term "canon," see further below, 15–18.

Christian reader, who simply takes the NT for granted. Its place within Christianity is so prominent and longstanding that most will find it nearly impossible to imagine a Christianity without a NT. But just for this reason it needs to be emphasized that the NT was not an original or even a particularly early feature of Christianity. Rather, the NT developed only gradually over the course of several centuries, as the result of a complex variety of conditioning factors in the life of the ancient church, and did not attain the form in which we know it until the late fourth century. During the first and most of the second century, it would have been impossible to foresee that such a collection would emerge. Therefore, it ought not to be assumed that the existence of the NT is a necessary or self-explanatory fact. Nothing dictated that there should be a NT at all. Furthermore, even when the idea of such a collection took hold, it remained for a long time uncertain what its substance and shape would be, and it might have taken any number of different forms than the one it ultimately acquired. Many possibilities were open.[2] So, just as the existence of a NT was not foreordained, neither were its contents. And our familiarity with the NT should not blind us to the genuine peculiarities of its substance: for example, that it contains four Gospels instead of only one (especially when the first three are so similar and the fourth so different); or that it contains so many letters of Paul but so few of any other writer; or that it contains only one prophetic book (Revelation) and only one historical book (Acts). It is not obvious why the NT embraces just these documents and not others—when there were many others which could have been included—or why, conversely, it contains as many and various documents as it does.

While the formation and significance of the NT canon have attracted the interest of NT scholars, in the field of NT studies as a whole these problems have not had very high billing.[3] The scholarly study of the NT has traditionally been preoccupied with the individual documents which belong to the canon and has dealt primarily with questions of

2. For a review of the alternatives, each of which was not only possible but had some embryonic development in early Christianity, see Adolf von Harnack, *The Origin of the New Testament* (New York: Macmillan Co., 1925), 169–78.

3. The most fertile period of canon studies was the late nineteenth and early twentieth centuries: Theodor Zahn, *Geschichte des neutestamentlichen Kanons*, 2 vols. (Erlangen, 1888–92); B. F. Westcott, *A General Survey of the History of the Canon of the New Testament*, 6th ed. (Cambridge, 1889); J. Leipoldt, *Geschichte des neutestamentlichen Kanons*, 2 vols. (Leipzig, 1907–8); Harnack, *Origin of the NT*. All these remain standard works.

their authorship, historical and religious background, literary character, theological ideas and purposes. By comparison with this concentration on the discrete contents of the NT, relatively little attention has been paid to the canon itself, and to this extent the canon has been taken for granted even in NT scholarship.[4]

Recently, however, the canon has emerged as a focal point of scholarly concern, and it is not much of an exaggeration to say that today the canon is among the leading topics of NT studies. This renewed interest in the canon is due to many factors. These include modern discoveries of early Christian literature previously unknown or known only at secondhand, new appraisals of the history of the OT canon and its bearing on the formation of the NT canon, and a heightened awareness of the variegations and conflicts of early Christianity. Some stimulus has come also from modern ecumenical discussion, which has brought into clearer focus the divergent conceptions and uses of the canon in the various branches of Christianity. But above all, questions about the canon have been posed by the interpretation of the NT writings themselves. Ironically, *the more fully the individual documents of the NT have been understood, the less intelligible the NT as a whole has become,* both historically and theologically.

On the historical side, exegesis has emphasized the highly occasional character of the writings contained in the NT: each emerged in a particular historical setting, dealt with specific issues of the moment, and was directed to a limited and often strictly local readership. This recognition poses very sharply the questions of how, why, and with what results these writings were detached from their generative contexts, brought together in a collection, and ascribed a general relevance and timeless authority for Christianity as a whole. Further, the historical study of the NT has steadily undermined the traditional legitimations of the canon (e.g., that these writings were composed by apostles, or that they are distinguished by their inspiration). Examined within the full context of early Christian literature, the documents which came to constitute the NT canon are not, as a group, recognizably unique.

4. This results partly from increasing disciplinary specialization which has led to an unfortunate separation between NT studies and early church history. It is no accident that the two most recent major studies are by scholars better known as church historians than as NT specialists: Robert Grant, *The Formation of the New Testament* (New York: Harper & Row, 1965) and Hans von Campenhausen, *The Formation of the Christian Bible* (Philadelphia: Fortress Press, 1972). Symptomatically, many NT "Introductions" contain no discussion of the formation or significance of the canon.

On the theological side, the NT canon has become, if anything, still more problematical. The religio-historical interpretation of the NT has led inexorably to the insight that among its contents there is an astonishing variety of theological assumptions and perspectives. This inner diversity manifests itself in fundamental tensions and, some would say, outright contradictions of a theological sort within the boundaries of the NT. This state of affairs must not be given a hasty or facile explanation, as though it were a matter merely of different idioms or of natural (and thus negligible) results of situational differences. Rather, one must reckon with the fact that the NT incorporates various independent and to some extent heterogeneous conceptions of the very meaning of Christianity. Like the recognition of historical diversity within the NT, sensitivity to its theological diversity stirs interest in the history of the canon, but it also raises far-reaching questions about the nature of the canon as a theological norm. In particular, how can the NT possess and exercise the religious authority traditionally vested in it when it increasingly seems to lack theological consistency among its own contents?

Finally, the historical-critical exegesis of the NT has resulted in a highly ambiguous relationship between the phenomenon of the canon and the tasks of exegesis. On the one hand, the essential and traditional subject matter of exegesis has been stipulated by the canon. It is precisely their presence in the canon which has not only insured that these writings have survived and can still be studied but has also endowed them with the religious authority which has constituted their special interest as objects of detailed and specialized interpretation. In these ways exegesis presupposes the canon. But on the other hand, so far as the aim of exegesis has been to gain a fully historical comprehension of the NT literature, the canon is only an obstacle to be overcome because it serves to obscure the original historical contexts and relationships to which its contents first belonged. Consequently, the interpreter of the NT is driven outside the canon in order to make sense of the documents within the canon, and this suggests that the canon as such has little bearing on the interpretation of its contents. This awkward situation—in which the canon sets the agenda for exegesis yet exercises slight influence on exegesis—points up the need to reconsider the hermeneutical function of the canon and to clarify the relationship between the canon, the contents of the canon, and the tasks of exegesis.

14

INTRODUCTION

SOME IMPORTANT TERMS

Canon[5]

The English word "canon" is a transliteration of the Greek *kanōn*, which had a rich history in ancient usage, both secular and early Christian. Its meaning as a designation of an authoritative collection of writings can be estimated only against this background. The Greek *kanōn*, along with its cognates, was formed on the Semitic root *kane*, meaning a "reed" (of bulrush or papyrus; cf. English "cane"). *Kanōn* also signified a reed, especially the reed as a tool for measurement or alignment, and therefore acquired the basic sense of "straight rod." In this sense the word had a special currency in the field of craftsmanship, where it meant "measuring rod" or "ruler," or any other tool whose purpose was to establish or to test straightness (e.g., a level, a plumb line). From this literal sense there arose metaphorical applications of the term: *kanōn* came to mean also a "norm," an ideal standard, a firm criterion against which something could be evaluated and judged. In this broader, metaphorical sense, the word *kanōn* was used in a variety of contexts, including art, music, literature, ethics, law, and philosophy. So, for example, Pliny the Elder spoke of Doryphoros as the canon in sculpture; Aristotle regarded the good man as the canon in ethics; Epicurus considered logic as the canon of true knowledge. In these cases it is the abstract sense of *kanōn* as "norm" or "standard" which is uppermost. But the word *kanōn* also had another and rather distinct meaning in antiquity, namely "list," "catalogue." This sense of the word seems also to have been derived from its basic meaning of "measuring rod" but had its point of departure in the calibrated marks on such a tool, which gave rise to the idea of a fixed series. Hence, an arithmetic table, a catalogue of astronomical observations, or an outline of chronological events might be called a *kanōn* in the sense of an established list.

Early Christianity first took up the word "canon" in its metaphorical sense of "norm" but not in connection with written materials. Its earliest occurrences in Christian usage are in two passages in the letters of Paul. In Gal. 6:16 Paul pronounces a benediction, "Peace and mercy be upon all who walk by this *kanōn*. . . . ," that is, this "rule" or "norm," and clearly it is the gospel message which Paul holds out as

5. For full discussions of this term, see esp. H. Oppel, *KANON: Zur Bedeutungsgeschichte des Wortes und seiner lateinischen Entsprechungen (regula, norma)*, Philologus Sup. 30, 4 (Leipzig, 1937); Theodor Zahn, *Grundriss der Geschichte des neutestamentlichen Kanons* (Leipzig, 1904), 1–14; H. W. Beyer, "Kanon," *TDNT* 3 (1965): 596–602.

a standard of living. In the second passage, 2 Cor. 10:13–16, the word *kanōn* occurs three times, but here its precise sense is not easy to determine. The following translation is given by the RSV:

But we will not boast beyond limit, but will keep to the limits [*to metron tou kanonos*] God has apportioned us, to reach even to you. For we are not overextending ourselves, as though we did not reach you; we were the first to come all the way to you with the gospel of Christ. We do not boast beyond limit, in other men's labors; but our hope is that as your faith increases, our field [*ton kanona*] among you may be greatly enlarged, so that we may preach the gospel in lands beyond you, without boasting of work already done in another's field [*en allotriō kanoni*].

Like the RSV, many translators and commentators take the word *kanōn* here as a geographical reference to the region of missionary work allotted to Paul. Although this seems to yield an adequate sense, such a meaning of the word is very poorly evidenced elsewhere.[6] Therefore, it is better to take the term in this context as a reference to Paul's mandate as apostle to the Gentiles, understood as the "norm" of his missionary work. This interpretation gives a greater consistency to Paul's use of the term, since both here and in Gal. 6:16 it would designate as the fundamental norm the gospel as it is actualized in the Pauline missionary preaching.[7] Apart from these Pauline texts, the word *kanōn* is found elsewhere in first-century Christian literature only in *1 Clement*, composed about 96, where it refers to "rules" governing moral behavior and ecclesiastical practice.[8]

In the late second century, however, the Christian use of the term *kanōn* became much more common. It regularly appears in such phrases as "the rule of truth" (*ho kanōn tes alētheias*, or the Latin equivalent, *regula veritatis*) and the "rule of faith" (*ho kanōn tēs pisteōs; regula fidei*), phrases which typically refer to summary formulations of Christian belief, understood as the norm or standard to which teaching, faith, and practice ought to conform. More comprehensive still are the phrases "the rule of the Church" (*ho kanōn tēs ekklēsias*) or "the ecclesiastical rule" (*ho ekklēsiastikos kanōn*), which refer to the whole of Christian teaching together with such authorities, regulations, and actions as are prescribed by and effective within the church.[9] Thus,

---

6. But see J. F. Strange, "2 Corinthians 10:13–16 Illuminated by a Recently Published Inscription," *BA* 46 (1983) 167–68.

7. See E. Käsemann, "Die Legitimät des Apostels. Eine Untersuchung zu 2 Korinther 10–13," *ZNW* 41 (1942):33–71, esp. 56–61; Beyer, "Kanon," 599; and see I. Lönning, *Kanon im Kanon: Zum dogmatischen Grundlagenproblem des neutestamentlichen Kanons*, Forschungen zur Geschichte und Lehre des Protestantismus 43 (Oslo: Universitetsforlaget, 1972), 17–23.

8. The passages are *1 Clement* 1.3; 4.1; and 7.2.

9. See, e.g., Irenaeus, *A.H.* 1.9.4; 1.10.1; 5.20.1; *Demonstratio* 3; Tertullian, *Praescriptio* 13, 27; *De virginibus velandis* 1; Clement, *Strom.* 7.15.90 and in Eusebius, *H.E.* 6.13.3.

by the late second century and thereafter, the word *kanōn* served to designate what the church acknowledged as having regulative authority for its faith and life.

It is important to notice that the word "canon" did not begin to be applied to Christian *writings* until the mid-fourth century. The earliest known use of the term in this connection is furnished by Athanasius, bishop of Alexandria, in his *Decrees of the Council of Nicea*, written soon after 350. There he describes the document known as *The Shepherd of Hermas* as "not of the canon" (*mē ōn ek tou kanonos*). Somewhat later, in his famous Easter Letter (*Ep*. 39) of 367, he provides a list of authoritative early Christian writings and describes them as "canonical" (*kanonizomena*). About the same time the Council of Laodicea (ca. 360) refers to the "uncanonical" (*akanonista*) and the "canonical" (*kanonika*) books of the old and new covenants. Subsequently it became common to use the term "canon" for the collection of authoritative books. But there is room for some uncertainty about exactly what the word meant when it was used in this way. Th. Zahn argued that in this connection "canon" had the simple sense of "list" or "catalogue" and did not signify that the writings so designated possess normative authority.[10] Others, however, have maintained that the designation of a collection of books as "canon" is of a piece with the earlier Christian use of the word and that "what really counted was the concept of norm inherent in the term," so that these writings are to be understood as containing the "canon of truth," the basic, authoritative teachings of Christianity.[11] The philological evidence decisively favors the view of Zahn: as applied to a group of writings, "canon" first of all meant simply a "list," specifically a list of those writings generally employed in the church, and most especially those customarily read in public worship.[12] Thus, the term served mainly to signify the actual use to which these writings were put and not to impute a peculiarly regulative authority to them.[13]

Though it is important to make this distinction, it cannot be absolutized. The writings which were included in the "list" (or canon) were

10. Zahn, *Grundriss*, 8ff. See also A. Souter, *The Text and Canon of the New Testament*, rev. ed. by C. S. C. Williams (London: Duckworth, 1954), 141–43.

11. Beyer, "Kanon," 601. See also W. Schneemelcher, "Canonical and Apocryphal," in *New Testament Apocrypha*, trans. and ed. R. McL. Wilson (Philadelphia: Westminster Press, 1963), 1:24.

12. This usage is well attested in secular Greek, and the subsequent applications of the term in other aspects of church life are mostly indebted to the formal sense of "list." See G. Lampe, *A Patristic Greek Lexicon* (1961), 701.

13. Similarly, the term *apocrypha*, meaning "hidden away," was applied to writings not publicly read in worship but only used privately. On the history of the term see A. Oepke, "Krypto," *TDNT* 3 (1965):997–1000, and Schneemelcher, "Canonical and Apocryphal," 24–27.

widely acknowledged as authentic and authoritative and could find a place in the list of books used in worship precisely because of this general recognition of their character. Hence, even if it was not originally intended by speaking of these documents as "canonical" in the sense of being "in the list," the idea of their normative status inevitably came to be connoted by the term "canon," and all the more since in previous Christian usage the word had consistently had the sense of "norm" or "standard," albeit in other connections entirely.[14]

Scripture

If in connection with Christian writings the word "canon" originally had the specific sense of a fixed list of authoritative documents, the term "scripture" designates writings which are taken to be religiously authoritative and are used and valued as such, yet without regard to their systematic enumeration or limitation. Whereas the concept of canon presupposes the existence of scriptures, the concept of scripture does not necessarily entail the notion of a canon. It is entirely possible to possess scriptures without also having a canon, and this was in fact the situation in the first several centuries of Christianity.[15]

But how does a document become scripture? None of the writings which belong to the NT was composed as scripture, for in the first century, specifically Christian scriptures were scarcely even thought of: "the scriptures" for earliest Christianity were invariably the Jewish scriptures. The documents which were eventually to become distinctively Christian scriptures were written for immediate and practical purposes within the early churches, and only gradually did they come to be valued and to be spoken of as "scripture." The crucial factor in this development was, quite simply, the utility of these writings within Christian communities. That is, certain writings were found to be specially helpful in sustaining, enriching, renewing, and directing the faith and life of the churches. As a result, those writings came to be valued and widely employed in Christian worship and teaching alongside the Jewish scriptures and in some ways proved even more useful than the Jewish scriptures. It was on the basis of this sustained experience of their usefulness that the church recognized them as con-

14. See Lönning, *Kanon im Kanon*, 27–29. The ambiguity between the functional and formal senses of the term "canon" ("norm" vs. "list") has been carried over into modern discussions, often with confusing results. The authoritative citation of a document does not signal its canonicity in the strict and formal sense of inclusion in a fixed list. The distinction is properly emphasized by A. C. Sundberg, Jr., "Toward a Revised History of the New Testament Canon," *StEv* 4 (=TU 102; Berlin, 1968), 452–61, and idem, IDBSup, s.v. "Canon of the NT."

15. See J. Barr, *The Scope and Authority of the Bible* (Philadelphia: Westminster Press, 1980), 120.

stituting "scripture." Religious authority was not simply intrinsic to the documents themselves; it emerged within and was contingent on the church's recognition of their creative and corrective effects on its own life.

New Testament

It remains to examine the term "New Testament," by which the canon of early Christian literature is traditionally titled.[16] "New Testament" is a latinized rendering of the Greek "new covenant" (*kainē diathēkē*). As employed in earliest Christianity, "new covenant" did not refer to a collection of Christian writings. Instead, it served to characterize the new order of salvation inaugurated by the Christ event, in correlation and contrast with the "old covenant" of God with Israel.

While the concept of a "new covenant" of God with his people originated in Israelite prophecy (Isa. 55:3, 61:8; Jer. 31:31, 32:40; Ezek. 16:60), its application to the Christian revelation seems to have emerged in connection with the death of Jesus, understood as a sacrificial spilling of blood to seal a covenant relationship (cf. Exod. 24:8). In the earliest eucharistic tradition available to us, Paul attributes to Jesus the saying, "This cup is the new covenant in my blood" (1 Cor. 11:25), and words to a similar effect occur in the Gospel accounts of the last supper (Matt. 26:28; Mark 14:24; Luke 22:20, but only Luke gives the adjective "new"). Paul also uses the phrase in 2 Cor. 3:6, describing the apostles as "ministers of a new covenant, not in a written code but in the Spirit; for the written code kills, but the Spirit gives life." The association to which Paul alludes between the "old covenant" and a "written code" recurs in the following context as Paul alleges that "when [the Jews] *read the old covenant,* that same veil [which Moses wore (Exod. 34:29–35)] remains unlifted, because only through Christ is it taken away" (2 Cor. 3:14, *italics added*). Here Paul speaks of the old covenant as something written and read (cf. 3:15, "whenever Moses is read"), but what he has in mind is not the OT as a whole but simply the law of Moses, the reading from which was a fixed part of the synagogue service. But if the old covenant was thus seen as having a literary component, this was not true of the new covenant, and Paul is concerned to emphasize precisely this dissimilarity, among others, when he contrasts the written code and the Spirit. It may be added that in the only other early Christian text where the conception of

---

16. See the discussions by W. C. van Unnik, "*He Kaine Diatheke*—A Problem in the Early History of the Canon," *StPat* 4 (=TU 79; Berlin, 1961), 212–27, and Campenhausen, *Formation,* 262–68.

Christianity as a new covenant receives any elaboration—namely, the Epistle to the Hebrews—it is apparent that the phrase does not entail any thought of written materials.

This absence of any association between the idea of a new covenant and Christian writings persisted for a long time.[17] Even in the late second century, Irenaeus, bishop of Lyons, who made very full use of the covenant concept and had the highest appreciation of Christian scriptures, did not make a close correlation between the two. For him, covenant remains a purely theological concept which cannot be reduced to or reserved for documents. Still, the application of covenant terminology to Christian writings must have begun in the late second century. According to Eusebius (*H.E.* 4.26.14), Melito, bishop of Sardis (ca. 170–90) spoke of a list of "the books of the old covenant," referring in this way to Jewish scriptures. But this does not necessarily imply that he had a parallel concept of "books of the new covenant," as has sometimes been supposed. The purpose of a list of "books of the old covenant" was to assure that proof texts drawn by Christians from the Jewish scriptures would be taken from writings recognized as authoritative by Jews, for otherwise the proofs would carry no weight. But this purpose had no relevance to Christian writings. Some importance has occasionally been seen also in the remarks of a late second-century, anti-Montanist writer who, according to Eusebius (*H.E.* 5.16.3), expressed his reluctance to compose a treatise against the Montanists

from timidity and scruples, lest I might seem to be adding to the writings or injunctions of the word of the new covenant of the gospel, to which no one who has chosen to live according to the gospel itself can add, and from which he cannot take away.

Some have seen here the earliest application of the title "new covenant" to a fixed collection of Christian writings,[18] but this is neither clear nor probable.[19] Rather, it is first with Clement of Alexandria (ca. 180–200) that the term "covenant" is brought into a strict relation with authoritative Jewish and Christian scriptures.[20] His successor, Origen,

17. E. Ferguson, "The Covenant Idea in the Second Century," in *Texts and Testaments: Critical Essays on the Bible and Early Christian Fathers,* ed. W. E. March (San Antonio, Tex.: Trinity Univ. Press, 1980), 135–62.
18. W. C. van Unnik, "De la regle *mete prostheinai mete aphelein* dans l'histoire du canon," *VC* 3 (1949): 1–36, followed by Campenhausen, *Formation,* 265.
19. Van Unnik himself has withdrawn the suggestion in "*He Kaine Diatheke,*" 217–18.
20. *Strom.* 1.9.44; 3.11.71; 4.21.134; 5.13.85, etc.

speaks still more explicitly about "the divine scriptures of the so-called old and so-called new covenant,"[21] though Origen's phraseology here suggests that he regarded such terminology as novel and perhaps not wholly suitable. Yet it is evident also that the writings are not themselves the covenant; they merely pertain to it and serve to document it.

The effort of Latin Christianity to adopt this conception of scriptures as testimony to the covenant of God with his people was accompanied by a variation of translation and ultimately by a distortion of meaning. Tertullian of Carthage (ca. 200), the first Latin Christian writer to use such terminology, sometimes renders the Greek *diathēkē* (covenant) with the Latin word *testamentum*, but he himself apparently preferred to translate it with *instrumentum*.[22] Nevertheless, it was the Latin phrase *novum testamentum* which took hold and persisted in Western usage. In purely lexical terms the translation of "new covenant" by *novum testamentum* is correct, since *testamentum* is the Latin equivalent of the Greek *diathēkē*: in ordinary usage each meant "[last] will and testament." But conceptually this was a mistake, for in biblical Greek *diathēkē* had *not* been used in this sense but with the meaning "covenant" or "compact," representing the Hebrew *berith,* for which the normal Greek equivalent would have been *synthēkē* rather than *diathēkē*. As a result, the Latin *testamentum* misses entirely the fundamental theological meaning of the biblical notion of covenant and misconstrues the relation of the scriptural writings to it. The ruling idea is no longer that these are the scriptures that pertain to the covenant but rather that these scriptures constitute God's testament— that is, the final and authoritative statement of the divine will, on the order of the "last will and testament" of a human person. This shift had the unfortunate consequence of fostering a wooden and juridical view of the scriptures as the full repository of revelation and the definitive expression of the divine will.

Viewed in terms of its actual development, the title "New Testament" should be understood to mean "books pertaining to the new

---

21. *Commentary on John* 5.8; *De principiis* 4.1.1, etc.

22. Tertullian uses *testamentum* sparingly but *instrumentum* very frequently. Yet he was aware that *testamentum* was the more usual and popular term (*Adv. Marc.* 4.1). For Tertullian these words were not synonymous, as Harnack has shown (*Origin of the NT,* 209–17). For a thorough examination of Tertullian's usage, see R. Braun, *"Deus Christianorum." Recherches sur le vocabulaire doctrinal de Tertullian* (Paris: Études Augustiniennes, 1962), 463–73. *Instrumentum* was a legal term for a document composed in properly legal form. In reference to Christian writings it suggested that they were fundamental and decisive for the exposition of Christian teaching.

THE NEW TESTAMENT CANON

covenant." The writings themselves are not the covenant but only witnesses to it. Furthermore, since the phrases "old covenant" and "new covenant" did not acquire a literary application until the late second century, well after the collection of Christian scriptures had begun to take shape, it is clear that in its origins the collection had nothing to do with the biblical covenant idea.[23]

23. Philip Vielhauer, *Geschichte der urchristlichen Literatur* (Berlin: Walter de Gruyter, 1975), 777.

22

II

The History of
The New Testament Canon

Since the ancient church left no record of how and why the NT was formed, the history of the canon must be reconstructed on the basis of sparse and fragmentary evidence and with a measure of conjecture. There are, generally speaking, three types of useful evidence. The first consists of the use of early Christian documents by Christian writers of the second through the fifth centuries. From the frequency and manner of their citations of and allusions to early Christian writings, it is possible to infer the value they attached to them. Uncertain and unsatisfactory as this procedure often is, such evidence is the best we have up to the end of the second century.[1] The second type of evidence is comprised by explicit discussions and judgments, either by individual writers or by ecclesiastical councils, about documents whose authority is either accepted or rejected. This evidence is very helpful but, with a few exceptions, belongs mostly to the fourth and fifth centuries. The third sort of evidence is provided by the contents of ancient manuscripts of the NT, together with some "scriptural aids" (concordances, prologues, etc.) variously included in them. This evidence, too, comes mostly from the fourth century and later, since not many extensive manuscripts have been preserved from the earlier period. The available evidence, interpreted carefully and with a view to the broader history of the ancient church, yields a coherent, if not particularly detailed, conception of the process by which the NT was formed.[2]

1. The mere fact that a document is quoted or alluded to by an early writer does not mean it had already attained canonical standing, even if it is called "scripture" or cited with some such formula as "it is written." See above 18 with n. 14 and, in addition, the remarks of Campenhausen, *Formation*, 103, and R. P. C. Hanson, *Tradition in the Early Church* (Philadelphia: Westminster Press, 1962), 205–8.
2. Useful collections of evidence are: E. Preuschen, *Analecta: Kürzere Texte zur Geschichte der Alten Kirche und des Kanons* 2, Zur Kanonsgeschichte, 2d ed. (Tübingen, 1910; repr. Frankfurt, 1968); E. Hennecke and W. Schneemelcher, ed., *NT Apocrypha*, 1:42–60; D. J. Theron, *Evidence of Tradition* (Grand Rapids: Baker Book House, 1957); Souter, *Text and Canon*, 188–220.

THE SECOND CENTURY

The Gospels

How, when and why the ancient church came to acknowledge four and only four Gospels is at many points obscure. Though it has sometimes been claimed that only these Gospels ever enjoyed general esteem and use in early Christianity, the evidence shows that the Gospels which eventually became canonical did not attain a clear prominence until late in the second century, and that even then their pre-eminence was neither universal nor exclusive. Furthermore, the Gospels did not become part of the NT canon individually. They were first shaped into a collection and then achieved canonical standing as a group. But the emergence of a four-Gospel collection was only the last stage of a long history of gospel traditions in the early church, and its significance can be appreciated only against that background.

It is uncertain just when traditions about Jesus, which were originally preserved by memory and transmitted by word of mouth, began to be committed to writing. The Gospel of Mark, written about 65, appears to have been the first full-blown narrative gospel, but its author undoubtedly drew on small written sources as well as on the fund of oral traditions. The authors of Matthew and Luke, besides making heavy appropriations from Mark and a written collection of sayings of Jesus (Q), also drew on other traditions, some of which were surely in written form. Beyond those represented in the Synoptic Gospels, others still were used by the author of John's Gospel, Thus, the last half of the century witnessed a rapid proliferation of documents embodying traditions about Jesus.

Some insights pertinent to the history of the canon can be gained from the very composition of these early Gospels. Source criticism has shown that the Gospel writers not only used existing written sources but also exercised great editorial freedom in adapting them. This makes it plain that the Gospel writers did not attach any special sanctity or even adequacy to their sources and that each meant to provide something better. This must have been the attitude of the authors of Matthew and Luke even toward the Gospel of Mark. Indeed, it was apparently the aim of each Gospel writer to offer an adequately comprehensive document which would stand on its own.[3] From this vantage point, a collection of Gospels is somewhat at odds with the aims of their authors. Further, redaction criticism has shown that each

---

3. This seems to be explicit, at least in the case of Luke (1:1–4): he aimed to compose the definitive account.

of the Gospels is an occasional document, produced in and directed toward a limited circle of readers and representing a particular theological interpretation of the Jesus traditions tailored to its own immediate context. Thus, each Gospel was at first *the* gospel document for an individual Christian community. In this light, the later estimate of these Gospels as mutually complementary and relevant to Christendom at large ignores their originally particular purposes and settings.

Although our canonical Gospels were among the earliest to be written, new gospels continued to be composed through much of the second century. Christian writers of the second century refer to many other gospels besides these four.[4] Modern manuscript discoveries have furnished us with texts of gospels previously known by name only (e.g., the *Gospel of Thomas* and *Gospel of Peter*) and have brought to light other gospel-type documents previously unknown (e.g., the *Dialogue of the Savior* and the *Apocryphon of John* found among the Nag Hammadi codices in 1945, or the so-called *Unknown Gospel* [Papyrus Egerton] published in 1935). Still other gospels mentioned by second- and third-century writers are no longer extant (e.g., the *Gospel of the Hebrews* and the *Gospel of the Egyptians*), and it is plausible that a fair number of other gospels which have failed to survive even in name were known and used in the early church. This rich multiplication of gospel literature indicates that in the first half of the second century the Gospels which we know as canonical were not recognizably unique and had not acquired special authority. At least their availability did not inhibit the ongoing production of similar documents. The currency of so many gospels also shows that the eventual development of a collection of only four Gospels was the result of a selective process. Nothing dictated that the church should honor precisely four Gospels, or these four in particular.

An early and interesting piece of external testimony about the Gospels is found in the remarks of Papias, bishop of Hierapolis in Asia Minor in the early decades of the second century, which have been preserved by Eusebius (*H.E.* 3.39.15–16):

And the presbyter used to say this: Mark became Peter's interpreter and wrote accurately all that he remembered, not indeed in order, of the things said or done by the Lord. For he had not heard the Lord, nor had he followed him, but later on, as I said, followed Peter, who used to give teaching as necessity

4. See H. Koester, "Apocryphal and Canonical Gospels," *HTR* 73 (1980): 107–12. For a collection of the extant texts, see Hennecke and Schneemelcher, *NT Apocrypha*, vol. 1.

demanded, but not making, as it were, an arrangement of the Lord's sayings, so that Mark did nothing wrong in thus writing down single points as he remembered them. For to one thing he gave attention, to leave out nothing of what he had heard and to make no false statements in them.

To this quotation from Papias, Eusebius immediately adds another: "Matthew collected the oracles [*logia*] in the Hebrew language, and each interpreted [translated?] them as best he could." The interpretation of these statements of Papias is immensely difficult, and many points are in dispute.[5] Papias seems clearly to have been acquainted with the Gospel of Mark. At the same time, the defensive tenor of his remarks implies that Mark was the object of some criticism, perhaps to the effect that it was incomplete or lacking appropriate arrangement. Such criticisms might have arisen when Mark was compared with another Gospel, but which? Papias would seem to provide the answer with his reference to Matthew, but it is uncertain whether he was thinking of our Matthew, which is not aptly described as a collection of *logia* and which was certainly not composed in Hebrew.[6] All that can be safely said on the basis of these comments is that Papias knew Mark and at least one other gospel-type document and that some comparative and critical discussion of them had taken place.

Equally interesting, however, is another statement which Eusebius attributes to Papias (*H.E.* 3.39.4):

If anyone ever came who had followed the presbyters, I inquired about the words of the presbyters, what Andrew or Peter or Philip or Thomas or James or John or Matthew, or any other of the Lord's disciples, had said, and what Ariston and the presbyter John, the Lord's disciples, were saying. For I did not suppose that information from books would help me so much as the word of a living and surviving voice.

So, although Papias knew written gospels, he did not defer to them but expressed a decided preference for oral tradition. This tradition was too well established to be completely displaced by written materials, and it continued to maintain a considerable authority alongside written gospels well into the second century. This is evident also from other Christian literature of the early second century which is collec-

5. The Papias fragments are conveniently collected and carefully discussed by W. R. Schoedel, *Polycarp, Martyrdom of Polycarp, Fragments of Papias*, The Apostolic Fathers 5 (Camden, N.J.: Thomas Nelson & Sons, 1967), 89–130.

6. Some have therefore taken Papias's statement as a reference to the synoptic sayings source (Q) on the assumption that it may have had some connection with the name Matthew. But this is wholly conjectural, and it is quite possible that Papias meant our Gospel of Matthew (thus Schoedel, ibid., 109–10). Apart from the problem whether Papias knew our Matthew, it has been variously supposed that he knew other Gospels as well. R. G. Heard, "Papias' Quotations from the New Testament," *NTS* 1 (1954): 130–34, points out that Papias cannot be shown to have depended on any of the Synoptic Gospels.

tively known as the "Apostolic Fathers." It has been shown that the citations of gospel-type traditions among the Apostolic Fathers are much more likely to have been drawn from the ongoing stream of oral tradition than to be free quotations from written gospels, to which no explicit appeals are made.[7] Hence, the reliance on oral tradition attested by Papias was not peculiar to him but was broadly typical in the first half of the second century, even though written gospels—including those which eventually became canonical—were already available. If the stubborn longevity and persistent authority of oral tradition checked the popularity of early written gospels, it also furnished a rich resource from which new gospel writings were derived. Both the *Gospel of Thomas* and the *Unknown Gospel* are independent redactions of oral tradition which owe nothing by way of form or content to the canonical Gospels,[8] and this may also be true for other gospel documents such as the *Gospel of Peter* and the *Dialogue of the Savior*.[9]

As oral tradition began to dissipate and grow wild, written gospels came increasingly into use. Originally, they circulated individually, and normally only one such document was valued and used in any given Christian community. Traces of this are still preserved. Some old manuscripts contain only one Gospel:[10] The textual tradition of Mark exhibits a much larger number of scribal corrections than those of other Gospels, and this may be due to a lengthier period of its individual circulation.[11] Marcion employed only one Gospel (Luke, or a form of Luke) in his collection of Christian scriptures, and although this is often set down to Marcion's theological bias, it probably reflects a common practice.[12] In any case, it was by no means assumed in the early second century that there was a need for more than one Gospel.

7. H. Koester, *Synoptische Überlieferung bei den apostolischen Vätern*, (= TU 65; Berlin: Akademie Verlag, 1957).

8. For the Gospel of Thomas, see H. Koester, "One Jesus and Four Primitive Gospels," *HTR* 61 (1968): 203–47 (= J. M. Robinson and H. Koester, *Trajectories Through Early Christianity* [Philadelphia: Fortress Press, 1971], 158–204) and H. Montefiore and H. E. W. Turner, *Thomas and the Evangelists*, SBT 35 (London: SCM Press, 1962). For the *Unknown Gospel*, see G. Mayeda, *Das Leben-Jesu-Fragment Papyrus Egerton 2 und seine Stellung in der urchristlichen Literaturgeschichte* (Bern: Haupt, 1946).

9. See Koester, "Apocryphal and Canonical Gospels."

10. P[52] and P[66] are the remains of second-century codices which contained only the Gospel of John. On the former, see C. H. Roberts, "An Unpublished Fragment of the Fourth Gospel in the John Rylands Library," *BJRL* 20 (1936): 45–55, and on the latter, see V. Martin, *Papyrus Bodmer II* (Geneva: Bibliothèque Bodmer, 1956) and *Papyrus Bodmer II, Supplement* (Geneva: Bibliothèque Bodmer, 1958).

11. G. D. Kilpatrick, *The Transmission of the New Testament and its Reliability*, Proceedings of the Victoria Institute 89 (1957), 96.

12. Cf. John Knox, *Marcion and the New Testament* (Chicago: Univ. of Chicago Press, 1942), 163–64.

Even when written gospels came into customary use, their authority was not absolute; indeed, their texts were not beyond substantial alteration. For example, Mark originally ended at 16:8 and so lacked any narrative of postresurrection appearances of Jesus. But at an early time, probably in the first decades of the second century, longer endings were variously added to the Gospel in order to remedy what was felt to be a deficiency, and the most common of these endings added twelve verses (vv. 9–20) which were subsequently taken up into most manuscripts and represented as integral to the text of Mark. Again, what we know as chap. 21 of John was not composed by the same person who wrote the rest of this Gospel. John 20:30–31 must have constituted the original conclusion, and chap. 21 was later added on, although this must have happened early—probably even before this Gospel entered general circulation, since no manuscript is known which does not contain chap. 21. Furthermore, the story of the woman taken in adultery which is ordinarily found in John as 7:53—8:11 was certainly no original part of the Gospel. Here is an instance where the text of a written Gospel has been expanded by the inclusion of a piece of oral tradition.[13] These are only striking illustrations of a more general tendency in the second century not to regard the texts of Gospels as sacrosanct but to subject them to revisions of various types.[14]

Through the circulation of individual Gospels, Christian communities gradually became acquainted with multiple documents of this type. The first evidence of a knowledge and use of several Gospels comes from the middle of the second century in the writings of Justin Martyr, who taught in Rome between 150 and 165. Justin was acquainted with Matthew and Luke and probably with Mark as well. (Although it has often been supposed that Justin also used John, this is at best uncertain and on the whole unlikely.)[15] Justin held these Gospels in high regard. Interestingly, he regularly designates them as "memoirs" or "reminiscences" (*apomnemoneumata*) of the apostles and those who followed

13. For the longer endings of Mark and the interpolation of John 7:53—8:11, see the concise discussions in Bruce Metzger, *A Textual Commentary on the Greek New Testament* (London: United Bible Societies, 1971); John 21 is fully discussed by R. E. Brown, *The Gospel According to John, XIII—XXI*, Anchor Bible (Garden City, N.Y.: Doubleday & Co., 1970), 1077–82.

14. See O. Linton, "Evidences of a Second-Century Revised Edition of St. Mark's Gospel," *NTS* 13 (1967): 321–55, and also M. Smith, *Clement of Alexandria and a Secret Gospel of Mark* (Cambridge: Harvard Univ. Press, 1973), arguing on the basis of a recently discovered letter of Clement that an expanded version of Mark was in use in Alexandria in the late second century.

15. J. N. Sanders, *The Fourth Gospel in the Early Church: Its Origin and Influence* (Cambridge: Cambridge Univ. Press, 1943), 31, and more recently M. R. Hillmer, "The Gospel of John in the Second Century" (Ph.D. diss., Harvard Univ., 1966), 51–73. Hillmer argues persuasively that there is no firm evidence for any relationship between Justin and the Gospel of John.

them.[16] With this characterization two features of Justin's attitude toward the Gospels stand out: he regards them as apostolic in origin (but
only indirectly so in the case of Luke and Mark), and he values them
chiefly as historical records, not as inspired scripture.[17] Justin also
remarks that in Christian services of worship it was customary to read
from both the "memoirs" of the apostles and from the "compilations"
of the prophets (*Apol.* 1.67.3). This does not mean that the Gospels
were authoritative in just the same sense as the prophetic writings;
for whereas Justin thinks the prophetic writings are inspired, he does
not value the Gospels in this way.[18] But his comment at least points
up the context in which the correlation of Jewish scripture and Christian writings gradually developed.

It is noteworthy that in spite of his knowledge of several Gospels,
Justin often cites traditions about Jesus which do not occur in these
Gospels and thereby betrays a familiarity with a broader body of materials which he did not hesitate to use. Even in his citations of sayings
of Jesus which do occur in these Gospels, there are some remarkable
variations, and these suggest that Justin did not quote written Gospels
directly. He seems at numerous points to have relied on oral tradition,
or on a compilation of sayings of Jesus, or perhaps on gospels not
known to us, or variously on all of these. Evidently Justin did not
invest any exclusive authority in the Gospels which ultimately became
canonical.[19]

The acquaintance of Christian communities with multiple Gospels
created some difficult problems. Individual Gospels had become lo-
cally well established and esteemed, and the traditional use of only
one such document militated against valuing more than one. Just as
each Gospel was composed in the first place with the aim of providing
a sufficient and self-contained account, it was not easy for Christian
communities to see why there should be more than one: a plurality of

16. *Apol.* 1:66.3; 1:67.3; *Dial.* 100.4; 101.3; 102.5; 103.6 and 8; 104.1; 105.1, 5 and 6; 106.1 and 4;
107.1. Only once does Justin apply the term Gospel to these writings (*Apol.* 1:66.3).

17. R. Grant, *The Earliest Lives of Jesus* (New York: Harper & Row, 1961), 14–20, with helpful
remarks on the meaning of *apomnemoneumata* in Greek and Christian antiquity. Cf. also N. Hyldahl,
"Hegesipps Hypomnemata," *StTh* 14 (1960): 70–113, esp. 77–83; and L. Abramowski, "Die 'Erin-
nerungen der Apostel' bei Justin," in *Das Evangelium und die Evangelien,* ed. P. Stuhlmacher
(Tübingen: Mohr Siebeck, 1983), 341–53.

18. That reading a document in the service of worship did not itself signify scriptural status is seen
in Eusebius, *H.E.* 4.23.11. On inspiration, see below, 71–72.

19. W. Sanday, *The Gospels in the Second Century* (London, 1876), 88–137, remains useful for
Justin's treatment of Gospel materials. See also A. J. Bellinzoni, *The Sayings of Jesus in the Writings
of Justin Martyr,* NovTSup 17 (Leiden: E. J. Brill, 1967), who argues that Justin relied on a post-
Synoptic, harmonizing compilation of sayings of Jesus rather than on the Gospels themselves.

Gospels cast doubt on the adequacy of any.[20] This problem was compounded by the fact that the Gospels differ significantly among themselves, an insight that was by no means lost on the early church. Though some accounting might be given for these differences, to accept more than one Gospel was to be burdened with justifying their divergences.[21] Finally, the very word "gospel" had originally been a theological rather than a literary term in Christianity, designating the message of salvation, and in this sense it was obvious that there is only one gospel. This usage was so longstanding that when the word came to be secondarily applied to documents of a certain type—a development which occurred about the middle of the second century— there was understandable hesitancy to think in terms of numerous Gospels.

All these considerations help to explain one of the most notable phenomena in the early church's treatment of Gospel literature, Tatian's *Diatessaron*.[22] Tatian, a Syrian Christian who had studied with Justin in Rome, undertook about 170 to weave separate Gospels into one consecutive narrative. Since for this purpose Tatian employed mainly the Gospels of Matthew, Mark, Luke, and John, he is the earliest-known witness for the use of all four of these Gospels. Tatian's reliance especially on these may mean that by his time they were acquiring a special prominence within the larger field of gospel documents. They had not, however, attained fully authoritative standing. This is shown, on the one hand, by the fact that the *Diatessaron* embodies some traditions which are not derived from our Gospels, so that Tatian hardly regarded these four as uniquely or exclusively valuable.[23] On the other hand, Tatian's very free handling of these texts, which led him to destroy their literary integrity and freely recast their substance through transpositions, additions, and omissions, shows that he did not value these documents as individual—let alone sacrosanct—

20. O. Cullman, "The Plurality of the Gospels as a Theological Problem in Antiquity," in *The Early Church* (Philadelphia: Westminster Press, 1956), 39–54. For a useful collection of relevant texts see also H. Merkel, *Die Pluralität der Evangelien als theologisches und exegetisches Problem in der alten Kirche* (Berne: Lang, 1978).

21. For discussion of this problem in the ancient church, see H. Merkel, *Die Widersprüche zwischen den Evangelien. Ihre polemische und apologetische Behandlung in der alten Kirche bis zu Augustin*, WUNT 13 (Tübingen: Mohr Siebeck, 1971), and Grant, *Earliest Lives of Jesus*, 14–37, 52–62.

22. On the *Diatessaron* generally, see B. M. Metzger, *The Early Versions of the New Testament* (Oxford: Clarendon Press, 1977), 10–36, with reference to most of the relevant literature.

23. On the use of other materials than our four Gospels, see G. Messina, *Diatessaron Persiano* (Rome: Pontifical Biblical Institute, 1951) xxxv–lii; G. Quispel, "L'évangile selon Thomas et le Diatessaron," *VC* 13 (1959): 87–117; J. H. Charlesworth, "Tatian's Dependence upon Apocryphal Traditions," *HeyJ* 14 (1974): 5–17. While Tatian did not rely exclusively on our Gospels, it is not certain that he made extensive use of another gospel-type document, as has often been supposed.

writings but was interested only in their contents. Thus, the *Diatessaron* attests a still fluid situation in which multiple Gospels were known and used, but their separate existence was still felt as problematical. It is a telling fact that Tatian apparently encountered no criticism for his work; indeed, the *Diatessaron* enjoyed great popularity.[24] Its widespread use suggests that the problems posed by a multiplicity of gospel documents were felt in many areas of the ancient church.

The first evidence for a collection of our four Gospels, and the first attempt to assert its exclusive authority, is provided by Irenaeus, bishop of Lyons in Gaul, writing about 180. His remarkable statement about this collection deserves to be quoted at length:

It is not possible that the Gospels can be either more or fewer in number than they are. For, since there are four zones of the world in which we live, and four principal winds, and since the church is scattered throughout the whole world, and since the pillar and support of the church is the Gospel and the Spirit of Life, it is fitting that she should have four pillars breathing out immortality all over and revivifying men. From this it is evident that the Word, the Artificer of all, He that sits upon the cherubim and controls all things, has given us the Gospel under four aspects, but bound together by one spirit. . . . For the cherubim also were four-faced, and their faces were images of the dispensation of the Son of God. For the Scripture says, "The first living creature was like a lion," symbolizing his effective working, his leadership and royal power; the second was like a calf, signifying his sacrifice and sacerdotal order: "but the third had, as it were, the face of a man," an evident description of his advent as a human being; "the fourth was like a flying eagle," pointing out the gift of the Spirit hovering with his wings over the church. And therefore the Gospels are in accord with these things among which Jesus Christ is seated. . . . For the living creatures are quadriform, and the Gospel is quadriform, as is also the course followed by the Lord. For this reason were four principal covenants given to the human race, one, before the flood, under Adam; the second, after the flood, under Noah; the third, the giving of the Law, under Moses; the fourth, that which revives man and sums up all things by means of the Gospel. . . . These things being so, all who destroy the form of the Gospel are vain, unlearned and also audacious, those who represent the aspects of the Gospel as being either more in number than previously stated, or, on the other hand, fewer.

(*A.H.* 3.11.8–9)

Irenaeus's argument, which ingeniously adduces an allegorical interpretation of the four living creatures mentioned in Rev. 4:6–9 and alludes to four divine covenants, indicates that toward the end of the second century a collection of four Gospels was becoming current in the western region of Christianity. But his remarks also imply that this must have been something of an innovation, for if a four-Gospel collection had been established and generally acknowledged, then Ire-

24. Its far-reaching influence is documented by Metzger, *Early Versions*, 10–25.

naeus would not have offered such a tortured insistence on its legitimacy.

Another witness to the currency of a four-Gospel collection in the west is the Muratorian canon list, an annotated catalogue of authoritative books which seems to have been composed in the very late second or early third century.[25] The list is only partially preserved; it began with comments on each of the four Gospels, but the statements about Matthew and Mark are lost. What remains of its treatment of the Gospels may be quoted:

> . . . at which however he was present and so he has set it down.
> The third Gospel book, that according to Luke.
> This physician Luke after Christ's ascension,
> since Paul had taken him with him as a companion of his travels
> composed it in his own name
> according to his thinking. Yet neither did he himself
> see the Lord in the flesh, and thus as he was able to ascertain it,
> so he also begins to tell the story from the birth of John.
> The fourth of the Gospels, that of John [one] of the disciples.
> When his fellow disciples and bishops urged him he
> said: "Fast with me from today for three days, and
> what will be revealed to each one
> let us relate to one another." In the same night it was
> revealed to Andrew, [one] of the apostles, that,
> while all were to go over [it], John in his own name
> should write everything down. And therefore, though
> various rudiments are taught in the several
> Gospel books, yet that matters
> nothing for the faith of believers, since by the one guiding Spirit
> everything is declared in all: concerning the birth,
> concerning the passion, concerning the resurrection,
> concerning the intercourse with his disciples
> and concerning his two comings,
> the first despised in humility, which has come to pass,
> the second glorious in royal power
> which is yet to come. What
> wonder then if John so constantly
> adduces particular points in his epistles also,
> where he says of himself: What we have seen with
> our eyes and have heard with our ears and
> our hands have handled, these things we have written to you.
> For so he professes [himself] not merely an eye and ear witness,
> but also a writer of all the marvels of the Lord in order.

Lines 16–26 of this statement offer a defense of the four-Gospel collection. Specifically, it is urged that although the Gospels are indeed

---

25. The date and location have been recently disputed by A. C. Sundberg, Jr., "Canon Muratori: A Fourth Century List," *HTR* 66 (1973): 1–41. His arguments, though interesting, are not convincing. For criticism, see E. Ferguson, "Canon Muratori: Date and Provenance," *StPat* 18 (1982): 677–83. See Appendix for the full Muratorian canon list (au. trans.).

different, everything essential is present in each one, and this as a result of the guidance of the divine Spirit. The admission of the diversity among the Gospels, together with the claim that this diversity "matters nothing for the faith of believers," suggests that some had indeed found discrepancies troublesome and, perhaps for that reason, continued to prefer only one Gospel. The accompanying claim that each Gospel contains what is essential may well be a retort to a preference for one of the fuller Gospels (Matthew?), and/or possibly to a critical attitude toward Mark.[26] But if such issues still had to be addressed, then the four-Gospel collection had not yet become established beyond all objection. This is apparent especially from the treatment given here to the Gospel of John. The very elaborate justifications offered on its behalf (lines 9–16 and 26–34) cannot have been superfluous. Special pleading was required in this case, and the reasons for this can be found in the peculiar history of this Gospel in the second century.

The Gospel of John seems not to have been known or used by most second-century Christian writers, and to all appearances was first employed among gnostic Christians.[27] Basilides, a gnostic teacher in Alexandria (ca. 130) may well have cited it, and the Valentinian gnostic teachers Ptolemaeus and Heracleon (160–170) both wrote expositions of this Gospel.[28] Theirs are the earliest-known commentaries on the Gospel of John (or indeed on any early Christian writing), and the fact that they considered it worthy of such detailed study shows that John had acquired considerable standing in gnostic Christianity by the middle of the second century. By contrast, outside gnostic circles there was scant knowledge of or interest in John, and prior to the late second century no broad recognition of its authority. It is possible that the almost exclusively gnostic provenance of this Gospel through most of the second century militated against its more general acceptance. Beyond that, John also suffered from the use made of it by the so-called "new prophecy" movement, also known as Montanism, which flourished in the latter half of the second century. Its adherents claimed that the coming of the Paraclete promised in John (14:26, 15:26, etc.) had actually occurred in the person of Montanus, the founder of the

26. On these and related questions, see A. T. Ehrhardt, "The Gospels in the Muratorian Fragment," *Ostkirchliche Studien* 2 (1953): 121–38 (= *The Framework of the New Testament Stories* [Manchester: Manchester Univ. Press, 1964], 11–36).

27. The evidence is fully canvassed by Sanders, *Fourth Gospel*, and Hillmer, "Gospel of John."

28. For gnostic appropriations of John, see M. F. Wiles, *The Spiritual Gospel: The Interpretation of the Fourth Gospel in the Early Church* (Cambridge: Cambridge University Press, 1960), and E. Pagels, *The Johannine Gospel in Gnostic Exegesis*, SBLMS 17 (Nashville: Abingdon Press, 1973).

movement, and that the new Jerusalem foreseen in Revelation (21:2) would soon descend to earth. Opposition to the "new prophecy" sometimes entailed a critical attitude toward John. This is exemplified by the learned Roman churchman Gaius who, early in the third century, as a result of his distaste for Montanism, rejected both the Gospel and Revelation.[29] But perhaps the strongest reservations about John arose from the perception of its extensive differences from the other Gospels in both outline and substance. These discrepancies were problematical enough that some, rather than trying to rationalize them, found it easier simply to dismiss John from consideration altogether.[30]

Against this background it is not surprising that the author of the Muratorian list thought it necessary to give especially strong endorsements of John. These are offered in two claims. The first is embodied in an implausible legend about the origin of the Gospel (lines 9–16), the point of which is to assert that its authority is not of one apostle only but of all the apostles together![31] The second is the insistence, based on an appeal to the letter known as 1 John (1:1–3), that the author of the Gospel was a reliable eyewitness (lines 26–34).[32] By such means this Gospel is defended against its detractors. Yet so far as this was necessary, the four-Gospel collection itself could not be taken for granted.

Even though in the western regions of Christianity a four-Gospel collection was coming into its own near the end of the second century, the situation was not so fully developed elsewhere. In the same period, Clement of Alexandria, who knew and valued our four Gospels, still granted a good measure of authority to the *Gospel of the Hebrews* and the *Gospel of the Egyptians* and so did not hold exclusively to a collection of four Gospels.[33] From Syria there is a fascinating report pre-

29. See below, 51 with n. 73.

30. See the studies cited in n. 21 above. The idea, first attested by Clement of Alexandria (Eusebius, *H.E.* 6.14.7) but widely found thereafter (Wiles, *Spiritual Gospel*, 11–12), that John is the "spiritual Gospel" whereas the other Gospels deal only with the "outward facts," must have been conceived largely with a view to the great differences between John and the Synoptics, and in an effort to give them a positive explanation.

31. This legend (perhaps based on John 21:24) originally must have aimed to suggest that *only* John was authoritative among the Gospels because it alone had the backing of all the apostles. If so, it must have been devised when the Gospels were circulating individually and stood in competition with each other.

32. On this passage, see the remarks of Ehrhardt, "The Gospels in the Muratorian Fragment," 26–36. For the possible importance of the Johannine epistles for the reception of the Gospel of John, see R. Brown, *The Community of the Beloved Disciple* (New York: Paulist Press, 1979), 145–64.

33. J. Ruwet, "Clement d'Alexandrie: Canon des écritures et apocryphes," *Bib* 29 (1948): 77–99; 240–68; 391–408, esp. 396–401; and E. Molland, *The Concept of the Gospel in Alexandrian Theology* (Oslo: J. Dybwad, 1938).

served by Eusebius (*H.E.* 6.12.2) concerning Serapion, bishop of Antioch (ca. 190). In the community of Rhossus, which lay in Serapion's
jurisdiction, the *Gospel of Peter* was in use, and Serapion expressed
no reservation about this. But when it was eventually brought to his
attention that this Gospel might contain heterodox ideas, Serapion
banned its further use. The incident illustrates that a four-Gospel collection had not become normative in the east, and for several centuries
it was Tatian's *Diatessaron,* not a four-Gospel collection, which held
the field in the Syrian church.

In summary, our four canonical Gospels did not begin to acquire
clear prominence beyond oral tradition or among other written gospels
until the second half of the second century, first in the western area
of Christianity, and more slowly in the eastern. Even at the end of
the second century and in the west, the four-Gospel collection was
not so firmly established as has sometimes been thought, and problems
centered especially around John. It is also clear that, given the circumstances of second-century Christianity and the luxuriant variety of
gospel traditions, both written and oral, which were current during
that time, the formation of a four-Gospel collection was neither a necessary nor an entirely natural outcome of the history of gospel literature in the early church. It can only be seen as a compromise striking
a precarious balance between an unmanageable multiplicity of gospels
on the one hand and a single, self-consistent gospel on the other. The
nature of this compromise can be seen in the terminology applied to
the four-Gospel collection in late second-century sources. Writers of
this period tend still to speak of *the* gospel (singular) and in this way
both preserve the idea that "gospel" was originally a theological concept and not a book and emphasize the essential unity of the gospel.
Yet in connection with specific documents, they allow that this essential unity is distributed among four witnesses. These ideas are held
together and expressed by the formulation, "the Gospel *according to*
Mark," and so forth. Thus, there are not, strictly speaking, four Gospels but a fourfold gospel. In this way the tension between the need
felt for a single and unitary gospel and the actual presence of multiple
gospel documents is not overcome but perpetuated in the collection
of four Gospels.

The Letters of Paul

Of the twenty-seven documents which make up the NT, almost half
are letters ascribed to the apostle Paul. However large Paul's influence

35

may have been in earliest Christianity, his prominence in the NT canon is disproportionately larger. The peculiarity of this fact should not be overlooked. Paul was not a historical disciple of Jesus, and even after he became a Christian apostle he stood in an oblique relationship with the leading figures of the primitive church. Moreover, Paul's letters were practical expedients of his missionary work: addressed to specific churches, they are narrowly particular in substance and purpose and make no pretense of general interest or timeless relevance. How and why did they attain their standing in the NT?

The Early History of Paul's Letters

The early history of Paul's letters and the process by which they were collected are very obscure, and in the absence of any conclusive evidence several theoretical reconstructions have been proposed. A review of these will point up the main issues.

A traditional and widely held explanation may be called the "snow-ball theory." On this view, Paul's letters were highly valued from the outset by the communities to which the apostle wrote. After all, Paul was an authoritative figure to the churches of his founding, and even he takes note that some regarded his letters as "weighty and strong" (2 Cor. 10:10). If during his own lifetime Paul's letters were valued in his congregations, this may well have led to an exchange of his letters among such communities as possessed any, and thus to an ever wider circulation of them outside the churches to which they were first addressed. In this haphazard way, partial collections of the letters could have emerged in different localities until finally, by a process of accretion, all the letters would have been brought together and published as a group.

This explanation, while plausible in the abstract, rests on assumptions which may not be justified. Since each of Paul's letters was an ad hoc piece of correspondence written to a specific church and dealing with immediate and local issues, it is not obvious that an enduring value would have been seen in them even by their original recipients, much less by other churches. In fact, some letters of Paul were not preserved at all (cf. 1 Cor. 5:9; 2 Cor. 2:4), while others seem to have been preserved only fragmentarily (2 Corinthians is often thought to be made up of such fragments), and this indicates that Paul's letters were not always immediately appreciated or carefully treasured. If they had been in such early and general circulation as this theory alleges, it would be odd that the author of Acts, writing several decades after Paul's time, shows no knowledge of any letters of Paul and seems unaware that Paul even wrote letters.

In view of such problems, another theory was offered by E. J. Goodspeed.[34] He assumed that precisely because Paul's letters were occasional pieces of real correspondence they were not scrupulously preserved but, like all letters, were read and then laid aside only to be forgotten. In this way the silence of Acts about Paul's letters becomes explicable: according to Goodspeed, the letters, having fallen into disuse, were rescued from obscurity only *after* Acts was written, and indeed only *because* Acts was written. He conjectured that the publication of Acts, with its rehearsal of Paul's itinerary, prompted someone who was already acquainted with one or two of Paul's letters (Colossians and Philemon) to search out other letters of Paul among the Pauline churches mentioned in Acts. Having successfully retrieved these, the collector then wrote what we know as the letter to the Ephesians, intending it to be a summation of Paul's thought and an introduction to the collected letters. In this way Goodspeed accounted for the peculiar character of Ephesians, including its general cast, its resonance of other letters of Paul, its close literary relationship with Colossians, and its apparent pseudonymity. On Goodspeed's view, then, it was only through the labors of an ardent admirer of Paul that the apostle's letters escaped oblivion and were gathered up into a collection of nine authentic letters plus the pseudonymous Ephesians.

Despite its ingenuity, Goodspeed's theory has not been widely accepted, and for good reasons.[35] That Paul's letters immediately fell into obscurity is no less an assumption than the contrary view that they were continuously esteemed.[36] Also, it is a romantic notion that a single individual moved by personal admiration of Paul should have gone on an odyssey in search of "lost" letters of the apostle, and it seems unlikely that Acts played any role in this, since Acts nowhere intimates that Paul was a writer of letters. Further, recent studies of Ephesians, though granting that it is not an authentic letter of Paul, have shown that it is not merely a pastiche of themes from the genuine

---

34. Goodspeed, *New Solutions to New Testament Problems* (Chicago: Univ. of Chicago Press, 1927), 1–64; idem, *The Meaning of Ephesians* (Chicago: Univ. of Chicago Press, 1933); and many other publications.

35. The theory has been variously adopted and adapted mainly by Goodspeed's students: cf. John Knox, *Philemon Among the Letters of Paul*, rev. ed. (Nashville: Abingdon Press, 1959); A. E. Barnett, *Paul Becomes a Literary Influence* (Chicago: Univ. of Chicago Press, 1941); C. L. Mitton, *The Epistle to the Ephesians: Its Authorship, Origin, and Purpose* (Oxford: Clarendon Press, 1951) and *The Formation of the Pauline Corpus of Letters* (London: Epworth Press, 1955).

36. L. Mowry, "The Early Circulation of Paul's Letters," *JBL* 63 (1944): 73–86. Cf. Knox, *Philemon*, 71–72.

letters but must have its own specific historical setting and purpose. If Goodspeed were right about the introductory purpose of Ephesians, we would expect evidence that this letter once stood at the head of the collection, but the earliest known arrangements of the letters show nothing of the sort.[37]

Still another and no less ingenious explanation has been advanced by W. Schmithals.[38] He too supposes that the collector-editor of the Pauline letters was a single individual, but Schmithals attributes to him a very different motive: the purpose of the collector was to furnish the church at large with a useful weapon in its struggle against the gnostic tendencies which threatened Christianity in the late first and early second century. To this end he not only collected the letters but also edited them in order to depict the apostle as a constant and implacable foe of gnostic ideas. Schmithals is led to this conclusion by his supposition that virtually all the authentic letters of Paul (Galatians and Philemon excepted) are literary composites which have been editorially pieced together from diverse smaller letters and letter fragments. His theory about the origin of the Pauline collection is an effort to provide a historical context and unity of motive for the kind of thoroughgoing editorial work he detects in the letters. According to Schmithals, the editorial reworking of Pauline texts had two specific aims. First, it was necessary that each of Paul's letters be made to contain an element of anti-gnostic polemic, and since this was not always present it was supplied by combining different pieces of correspondence into new literary units. Second, the editor wished to consolidate the many fragments of Paul's correspondence into seven letters, so as to make clear by the symbolism of the number (seven = wholeness) that Paul's teaching was meant for the entire church. Thus, he fashioned a collection which was anti-gnostic in substance and catholic in shape. Hence, Schmithals reconstructs an original collection containing 1—2 Corinthians, Galatians, Philippians, 1—2 Thessalonians, and Romans.

Since Schmithals's theory is so fully predicated on his views about the composite character of individual letters, it must stand or fall with the plausibility of those views.[39] While most scholars are prepared to

37. C.H. Buck, "The Early Order of the Pauline Corpus," *JBL* 68 (1949): 351–57; see also below, 41–43.
38. Schmithals, "On the Composition and Earliest Collection of the Major Epistles of Paul," in *Paul and the Gnostics,* trans. J. Steely (Nashville: Abingdon Press, 1972), 239–74.
39. For Schmithals's redactional theories, see *Paul and the Gnostics* and *Gnosis in Corinth,* trans. J. E. Steely (Nashville: Abingdon Press, 1971).

grant that secondary editorial revision has affected some of the letters, Schmithals's analyses are suspect for their complexity, seeming arbitrariness, and sheer multiplicity, and few would agree with his estimates of the nature or extent of redaction among the Pauline letters. Furthermore, there is no good evidence that the collection ever contained only the seven letters he assigns to it or that they stood in the proposed order.[40] And if Paul's letters had been known and used beforehand, as Schmithals allows, it is difficult to imagine that an editor could have succeeded with such a promiscuous recasting as he alleges.

Both Goodspeed and Schmithals have sought to discover an occasion, an agent, and a motive for the formation of the Pauline letter collection by relying on features internal to the collection (pseudonymity and redaction). The same features are basic to yet another modern theory of the origin of the collection. H. M. Schenke has suggested that the collection of Paul's letters was the work of a "Pauline school," that is, a group of persons who knew and valued Paul's teaching and who assumed the responsibility for the continuation of Paul's work after the death of the apostle.[41] Schenke attributes to this group not only the gathering and preservation of authentic letters of Paul but also the editorial reworking of some of Paul's correspondence, the composition of "new" Pauline letters (Colossians, Ephesians, 2 Thessalonians, 1—2 Timothy, Titus), and the publication of the whole corpus. These various efforts were aimed at sustaining, extending, and developing Paul's teaching in his historic mission field after his death. Under this impetus the Pauline literary heritage gradually took shape, but since it was a matter of a living tradition of teaching, it remained pertinent for a time only to Pauline communities. The silence of Acts about letters of Paul is due to the fact that when Acts was composed the collection was still in its early stages and not generally known.

This is an attractive hypothesis in many ways. It recognizes that the development of the Pauline letter collection must be understood not merely in literary terms but as an aspect of the theological history of early Christianity: Paul's letters must have been preserved chiefly out of a persistent devotion to Paul's teaching. Further, this theory can make sense of the fact that the collection contains, along with authentic letters, both pseudonymous compositions and letters which have been editorially reworked, yet without relying on the dubious idea that a

40. H. Gamble, "The Redaction of the Pauline Letters and the Formation of the Pauline Corpus," *JBL* 94 (1975); 403–18.
41. "Das Weiterwirken des Paulus und die Pflege seines Erbs durch die Paulusschule," *NTS* 21 (1975): 505–18.

particular person was single-handedly responsible for all this. Of course, the existence of a "Pauline school" is an inference, but the continuing production of "Pauline letters," which show a deep indebtedness to Paul along with new developments and application to new circumstances, cannot be easily understood on any other basis. And since Paul had gathered around himself a group of associates who were instrumental in his missionary work, conversant with his thinking, and active in the supervision of his churches, it may be that such a group (or its successors) took up Paul's work after his death and sought all the more to preserve and extend his legacy.[42]

The mere presence within the collection of inauthentic and editorially revised letters shows that its formation was a creative endeavor, not merely a conservative one. It also has to be assumed that the history of the individual letters of Paul up to the formation of the collection was diverse. While some of the letters were lost, others were valued and circulated at any early time. Romans and 1 Corinthians were among these; the textual tradition shows that their original specific addresses were generalized early on, a change that must have been calculated to suggest their broader relevance and to promote their wider use.[43] It is probably not accidental that these two letters, along with Ephesians (which had no originally exclusive address), were the most widely known and cited in the early postapostolic period. Certainly the composition of pseudonymous letters after Paul's time presupposes that some of the authentic letters were in circulation, since otherwise a pseudonymous author could not expect that his "Pauline" letter would find ready acknowledgment and not seem anomalous in the circumstances.[44] Other letters of Paul, however, seem to have come into use only later. This was perhaps true of 2 Corinthians, and this would be comprehensible if, as many think, this letter was pieced together from smaller fragments of Paul's Corinthian correspondence. A satisfactory theory must give an account of

---

42. For the concept of a "Pauline school," see H. Conzelmann, "Paulus und die Weisheit," *NTS* 12 (1965): 321–44; but see also the criticism of B. Pearson, "Hellenistic-Jewish Wisdom Speculation and Paul," in *Aspects of Wisdom in Judaism and Early Christianity*, ed. R. L. Wilken (Notre Dame, Ind.: Univ. of Notre Dame Press, 1975), 43–66. For Paul's associates, consult E. E. Ellis, "Paul and his Co-Workers," *NTS* 17 (1971): 437–52; and W.-H. Ollrog, *Paulus und seine Mitarbeiter: Untersuchungen zu Theorie und Praxis der paulinischen Mission*, WMANT 50 (Neukirchen-Vluyn: Neukirchener Verlag, 1979).

43. N. A. Dahl, "The Particularity of the Pauline Epistles as a Problem in the Ancient Church," in *Neotestamentica et Patristica*, NovTSup 6 (Leiden: E. J. Brill, 1962), 261–71; and H. Gamble, *The Textual History of the Letter to the Romans*, SD 42 (Grand Rapids: Wm. B. Eerdmans, 1977), 115–24.

44. N. Brox, *Falsche Verfasserangaben: Zur Erklärung der frühchristlichen Pseudepigraphie*, SBS 79 (Stuttgart: Katholisches Bibelwerk, 1975), discusses conditions for the reception of pseudonymous writings.

THE HISTORY OF THE NEW TESTAMENT CANON

why some letters were lost, some preserved, some extensively edited, and some newly composed. It must also suggest a realistic context in which Paul's literary legacy was cultivated and finally codified in a formal collection. That the responsibility for this lay with a Pauline school is probable, for such a group furnishes just the sort of constituency which could have had the interest and the capacity for the task, and which would make intelligible both the diversity and the coherence of the Pauline letter collection.

Early Editions of the "Corpus Paulinum"

The collected letters of Paul must have been available by the late first century or early in the second. But the first solid evidence of an extensive collection is provided by Marcion near the middle of the second century, and it is not coincidental that Marcion is also the first Christian thinker of the second century with a deep theological indebtedness to Paul. Marcion's collection consisted of ten letters in the following order: Galatians, 1—2 Corinthians, Romans, 1—2 Thessalonians, Ephesians (which Marcion knew as "Laodiceans"), Colossians, Philippians, and Philemon.[45] Some have thought that Marcion was himself the first systematic collector of Paul's letters,[46] or at least that his arrangement of them reflects his own peculiar theological viewpoint, Galatians being placed at the head to emphasize the contrast and discontinuity between Christianity and Judaism.[47] But neither conjecture is likely. Marcion probably took over an existing edition of the collection without altering even its arrangement.

The nature of other early editions of the Pauline collection can be inferred from manuscripts, patristic writers, and canon lists of a somewhat later time.[48] These indicate that, besides Marcion's, there were two very old editions of the collection. In both of these the letters were arranged on the principle of decreasing length, but the same principle yielded two different results. When the letters to the same

45. The primary source for knowledge of Marcion's collection is Tertullian, *Adv. Marc.* 5.

46. W. Bauer, *Orthodoxy and Heresy in Earliest Christianity* (Philadelphia: Fortress Press, 1971), 221–22.

47. Ibid.; also Adolf von Harnack, *Marcion, Das Evangelium vom fremden Gott*, 2d ed. rev., (= TU 45; Leipzig: Hinrichs, 1924), 168*–69*; Knox, *Marcion*, 45–46; Campenhausen, *Formation*, 153 n. 22.

48. The most important recent studies are J. Finegan, "The Original Form of the Pauline Collection," *HTR* 49 (1956): 85–104; N. A. Dahl, "Welche Ordnung der Paulusbriefe wird vom muratorischen Kanon vorausgesetzt?" *ZNW* 52 (1961): 39–53; H. J. Frede, "Die Ordnung des Paulusbriefe und die Platz des Kolosserbriefs im Corpus Paulinum," in *Vetus Latina. Die Reste der altlateinischen Bibel* 24/2, Epistulae ad Philippenses et Colossenses (Freiburg: Herder, 1969), 290–303; and cf. N. A. Dahl, "The Origin of the Earliest Prologues to the Pauline Letters," *Semeia* 12 (1978): 233–77, esp. 262–63.

community (Corinthians, Thessalonians) were counted together as one length-unit, the resulting order was 1—2 Corinthians, Romans, Ephesians, 1—2 Thessalonians, Galatians, Philippians, Colossians (Philemon?). But when the letters to the same community were counted separately, the resulting order was virtually the one with which we are familiar: Romans, 1—2 Corinthians, Ephesians, Galatians, Philippians, Colossians, 1—2 Thessalonians (Philemon?). The former arrangement is probably the earlier. It seems to be based on the idea that Paul wrote to precisely seven churches, and a collection of that sort would, by the symbolism of the number, suggest its relevance to the church at large. If this was the underlying rationale, this edition did not contain the letters to Timothy and Titus and must have construed Philemon, another personal letter, as a companion to Colossians. The second arrangement was conceivably an independent early edition which simply offered thirteen letters of Paul without reference to the seven-churches concept; more probably it was derived from the seven-churches edition but departed from its rationale by counting separately letters to the same church and by adding the letters to Timothy and Titus.[49] It remains uncertain whether the collection attested for Marcion was another early, independent edition or was derived from the seven-churches edition. But in either case, the unusual order of the letters in Marcion's edition (with Galatians at the beginning) is better understood as an effort to present the letters chronologically than as the product of a dogmatic bias.[50] Thus, there is no good reason to think this arrangement had a Marcionite origin.

One traditional component of the Pauline collection was not regularly present in its early editions: namely, the pseudonymous letters to Timothy and Titus.[51] The first explicit witness to their presence in the collection is Irenaeus late in the second century. Prior to that time their status is unclear. They formed no part of Marcion's edition, doubtless because Marcion did not know them and not, as Tertullian alleged (*Adv. Marc.* 5.21), because he rejected them. They were not included in the old seven-churches edition of the letters, and they are not present in the earliest extant ms. of the Pauline corpus, P[46], which dates from the early third century.[52] Even in the Muratorian Frag-

49. Dahl, "The Origin of the Earliest Prologues," 262–63.
50. Frede, "Die Ordnung der Paulusbriefe," 295–96.
51. On Hebrews, see below, 47, 50, 52.
52. Some leaves are lost from the ms., but their number is insufficient to have contained the Pastorals. See F. G. Kenyon, *The Chester Beatty Biblical Papyri*, Fasc. 3, Supplement (London: Emery Walker, 1936), x–xi.

ment, these letters are described almost as an appendix to the collection and are given a separate justification. Hesitancy about the authority of these letters is understandable: since they were addressed to individuals, their relevance to the whole church was even harder to perceive than that of Paul's letters to particular churches. Here the problem of particularity, or a lack of "catholicity," was acute. This is also true of the little letter of Philemon, even though it seems to have belonged to the collection from the beginning, probably in association with Colossians. Though all four of these personal letters were part of the Pauline collection by the end of the second century, the legitimacy of this could be and was questioned as late as the fourth century.[53]

The Use of Paul's Letters in the Second Century

The collected letters of Paul were available in several editions early in the second century, but their use is not well evidenced until late in the second century.[54] Several writers belonging to the early decades of the second century were, however, acquainted with letters of Paul. Clement of Rome (ca. 96), Ignatius, bishop of Antioch (ca. 110), Polycarp, bishop of Smyrna (d. 155), and the author of 2 Peter (ca. 140?) allude to them, but it is impossible to tell how many letters each knew or whether they were acquainted with an extensive collection.[55] Only Polycarp among them offers clear quotations from Paul. Still, none of these writers shows an awareness or appreciation of distinctively Pauline teaching. What counts for them is not so much Paul's letters—and even less Paul's thought—as Paul himself, as an exemplary apostolic figure.[56] Other Christian writers of the first three-quarters of the second century seem even more innocent of a knowledge of Paul or his letters. Among the Christian apologists whose writings constitute the

53. Dahl, "The Particularity of the Pauline Epistles," 263–66.

54. Recent detailed surveys which come to similar results are A. Lindemann, *Paulus im ältesten Christentum. Das Bild des Apostels und die Rezeption der paulinischen Theologie in der frühchristlichen Literatur bis Marcion*, BHT 58 (Tübingen: Mohr Siebeck, 1978), and D. K. Rensberger, "As the Apostle Teaches: The Development of the Use of Paul's Letters in Second Century Christianity" (Ph.D. diss., Yale Univ., 1981).

55. Inferences based on their presumed allusions are quite various. See, e.g., D. A. Hagnar, *The Use of the Old and New Testaments in Clement of Rome*, NovTSup 34 (Leiden: E. J. Brill, 1973), 179–237; H. Rathke, *Ignatius von Antiochien und die Paulusbriefe* (=TU 99; Berlin: Akademie-Verlag, 1967); C. M. Nielsen, "Polycarp, Paul, and the Scriptures," *ATR* 47 (1965): 199–216. All argue for an extensive knowledge of Paul's letters among these writers. Much more limited acquaintance with Paul's letters is seen by W.Schneemelcher, "Paulus in der griechischen Kirche des 2. Jahrhunderts," *ZKG* 75 (1964): 1–20, and Bauer, *Orthodoxy and Heresy*, 216–21. Rensberger, "As the Apostle Teaches," is persuasive in claiming that Clement knew 1 Corinthians and Romans, that Ignatius knew 1 Corinthians and possibly Ephesians, but that Polycarp knew these three and five other letters besides.

56. Lindemann, *Paulus*, 71–97, 177–232.

bulk of second-century Christian literature, Paul is never mentioned by name, his letters are not cited, and there is no appropriation of his thought.[57] As a rule, then, Christian writers of this period are simply indifferent to Paul's letters. But this rule knows some striking exceptions.

The most important of these is Marcion, who was active near the middle of the second century. Marcion's entire understanding of Christianity was ostensibly based on Paul, whom he esteemed as the only true apostle of Christ. For him the letters of Paul, together with a version of the Gospel of Luke (which Marcion may have thought was derived from Paul), were the exclusively authoritative repository of Christian truth, and on the basis of these documents Marcion expounded and defended his ultra-Pauline conception of Christianity.[58] This teaching won many adherents but also evoked sharp criticism and by the late second century was broadly repudiated as heretical. Nevertheless, with Marcion, for the first time in second-century Christianity, Paul's letters are extensively employed as the scriptural resource and support of Christian teaching. In addition to Marcion, various gnostic Christian teachers of the second century advanced their interpretation of Christianity with the aid of Paul's letters. Basilides, who taught in Alexandria during the reign of Hadrian (117–138), and Valentinus, who probably came from Egypt but taught in Rome between 135 and 165, both made use of Paul's letters along with other early Christian writings. Among the followers of Valentinus a rather rich appeal was made to Paul's letters, especially by Ptolemy but also by Heracleon and Theodotus.[59] Apparently, gnostic Christians considered the apostle authoritative, yet not exclusively so, since they employed other writings to a similar effect.

The appeals made to Paul's letters by Marcion and the gnostic groups of the second century furnish a decided contrast to the neglect of Paul by other Christian writers during the same period. This state of affairs has evoked the opinion—widespread among modern scholars—that, because of the extensive appropriation of his letters by Marcion and the gnostics, Paul fell into disrepute among other Christians, and that before Paul's letters could become useful and authoritative for the

57. Justin is a striking example because of the larger body of his preserved writings and the likelihood that in Rome he would have gained a knowledge of the letters. Rensberger, "As the Apostle Teaches," 162–92, finds the evidence inadequate to decide whether Justin knew Paul's letters. Lindemann, *Paulus*, 353–67, thinks he did.
58. See the classic study by Harnack, *Marcion*. For Marcion's use of Paul's letters, see esp. Knox, *Marcion*, 39–76; Lindemann, *Paulus*, 378–90; and Rensberger, "As the Apostle Teaches," 149–62.
59. Lindemann, *Paulus*, 298–308; Rensberger, "As the Apostle Teaches," 134–40, 221–51.

church they first of all had to be rescued from the heretics.[60] On this view, Paul's ecclesiastical rehabilitation was accomplished in two ways: first, by adding to the Pauline collection the letters to Timothy and Titus, which depict an episcopal Paul concerned to establish authoritative teaching and to secure its proper transmission in the church; and second, by employing the Book of Acts, which integrates and indeed subordinates Paul in the larger apostolic ranks and so deprives him of autonomy and pre-eminence. But although the letters to Timothy and Titus and the Book of Acts do manifest these tendencies, it is difficult to imagine that they were composed with the intent of redeeming Paul from heretical use, however helpful they may have been in contextualizing the significance of Paul for the church.

Despite Paul's popularity among heterodox groups, it is not plausible that for this reason his letters were abandoned and only later reclaimed for general use.[61] No Christian writer of the second century shows any explicit animus toward Paul, except in Jewish Christianity, which was a heterodox movement. The fact that Paul's letters were not much used in second-century Christianity can be explained adequately on other grounds. The particularity of his letters was not easily overcome, for it was obvious that Paul had written to individual congregations and did not address Christians everywhere. Even at the end of the second century, this problem still had to be met. Thus, Tertullian reasoned, "What significance have the titles [of the letters]? What he says to one, he says to all" (*Adv. Marc.* 5.17). The author of the Muratorian fragment similarly urged the catholic relevance of Paul on the basis of the fact that Paul wrote to seven churches, "following the rule of his predecessor [!] John" who in Revelation "writes indeed to seven churches, yet speaks to all" (lines 48–9, 57–9).[62] Further, the general difficulty of understanding Paul, which is observed with some frustration in 2 Peter, coupled with the fact that many of Paul's concerns were not lively issues in second-century Christianity, must have posed strict limitations to Paul's usefulness. Also, indifference to Paul's letters in this period may be more apparent than real. Most of the

---

60. See, e.g., Bauer, *Orthodoxy and Heresy*, 212–28; Schneemelcher, "Paulus in der griechischen Kirche"; Campenhausen, *Formation*, 144–45, 177–81; C. K. Barrett, "Pauline Controversies in the Post-Pauline Period," *NTS* 20 (1974): 229–45; G. Strecker, "Paulus in nachpaulinischer Zeit," *Kairos* 12 (1970); Knox, *Marcion*, 114–39. For an etiology of this viewpoint, see Rensberger, "As the Apostle Teaches," 1–45.

61. It is a major contribution of Rensberger, "As the Apostle Teaches," to have shown this by careful examination of the source. Lindemann (*Paulus*, 402) is led to the same conclusion.

62. See Dahl, "The Particularity of the Pauline Epistles," and K. Stendahl, "The Apocalypse of John and the Epistles of Paul in the Muratorian Fragment," in *Current Issues in New Testament Interpretation*, ed. W. Klassen and G. F. Snyder (New York: Harper & Row, 1962), 239–45.

Christian literature of this era is apologetical, addressed to outsiders, and in this genre the use of specifically Christian authorities was not altogether suitable. With this it must be remembered that many of the same writers who do not appeal to Paul do not appeal much more to other Christian writings. Finally, if Paul's letters had been consistently disdained within the broader stream of Christian thought for most of the second century, then it would be very puzzling that they became suddenly well known and widely honored during the last two decades of that century. But the fact that Paul's letters are highly esteemed by Irenaeus, Tertullian, Clement of Alexandria, and the author of the Muratorian Fragment, geographically diverse as these witnesses are, implies that Paul's literary legacy had been more or less continuously and broadly valued during the preceding period as well, even if this is not readily apparent in the evidence that has been preserved.[63]

Other Writings

Many other Christian writings were also widely valued and employed during the second century, but only some of these were eventually to find their way into the NT canon. The fortunes of these documents illuminate the development of the canon, even in the case of those documents which were not finally included in it.

Although Revelation was written about 96, there are no clear traces of its use in the first half of the second century.[64] Our first direct witness to it is Justin Martyr (*Dial.* 81.15). In the west and nearer the end of the second century, Revelation was cited extensively by Irenaeus, and its currency in Gaul is shown also by the letter from the churches of Lyons and Vienne to the churches of Asia Minor preserved by Eusebius (*H.E.* 5.1). Tertullian quoted it and knew of none besides Marcion who did not accept it, thus showing its currency in North Africa. The Muratorian list also approves Revelation and even presumes on its authority to assert the catholicity of Paul's letters.[65] Thus, in the western regions of Christianity, Revelation was well known and much used by the late second century. Its currency in the east, however, was somewhat more limited. According to Eusebius, Melito,

63. Rensberger, "As the Apostle Teaches," 330–59, shows that the tendency in the second century was toward the ever greater and more explicit use of Paul's letters.
64. Still helpful for the history of this document in early Christianity is N. B. Stonehouse, *The Apocalypse in the Ancient Church* (Goes: Oosterbann & Le Cointre, 1929).
65. The opinion of Sundberg, "Canon Muratori," 21–26, that Revelation has only marginal status in the Muratorian list, is surely wrong.

bishop of Sardis (ca. 190), wrote a commentary on this book (*H.E.* 4.26.2), an effort presuming its authority, and Theophilus, bishop of Antioch (ca. 185), quoted it (*H.E.* 4.24.1, cf. *Ad Autolycus* 2.28), but otherwise we can be certain only that Clement of Alexandria used it. Later, however, Revelation came under dispute both in the west and in the east (see below, 51–52).

The Epistle to the Hebrews appears to have been used (though never named) by Clement of Rome in the last years of the first century, but during the second century it commanded almost no interest in the western church. Tertullian knew Hebrews and thought it was written by Barnabas, but he made scant use of it, appealing once to its teaching against a second repentance (*De pudicitia* 20). Neither Irenaeus nor the Muratorian list shows any awareness of this letter. In the east, by contrast, Hebrews must have been more consistently popular. By the late second century, Clement of Alexandria maintained its scriptural authority and thought that it was written by Paul, and in P[46], the earliest extant codex of Paul's letters (early third century), Hebrews stand firmly within the Pauline collection.[66]

The Acts of the Apostles, although composed as a companion piece to the Gospel of Luke, had a separate history from Luke and did not come into any broad currency until later.[67] Justin Martyr, near the mid-second century, is the first writer to show any knowledge of Acts (*Apol.* 2.50.12), but it was later still that any real importance was attached to Acts, possibly as a consequence of the conflicts with Marcion and gnostic groups. Something of the sort is suggested by the manner in which Irenaeus appeals to Acts as a proof of the unity of the apostles and their preaching. The authority of Acts for Irenaeus rests on the belief that its author was an inseparable companion of Paul and a disciple of the other apostles. The esteem acquired by Acts at the end of the second century is confirmed by the Muratorian list (lines 34–39), Tertullian, and Clement of Alexandria.

The so-called "catholic epistles" (James, 1 and 2 Peter, 1, 2, and 3 John, and Jude) were little used in the second century. Only 1 Peter and 1 John had much currency. Eusebius reports that Papias knew and used these two letters (*H.E.* 3.39.17) and that Polycarp used 1 Peter (*H.E.* 4.14.9, confirmed by Polycarp's letter to the Philippians).

66. C. P. Anderson, "The Epistle to the Hebrews and the Pauline Letter Collection," *HTR* 59 (1966): 429–38, argues that Hebrews may have been part of the collection from the beginning, but there is almost nothing to be said for this.

67. See the excellent survey of the evidence by E. Haenchen, *The Acts of the Apostles. A Commentary* (Philadelphia: Westminster Press, 1971), 3–14.

Nevertheless, even by the end of the second century, the use of these two letters remained sparing: Irenaeus and Tertullian make few appeals to them, while the Muratorian list observes that "two epistles with the title John are accepted in the catholic church" (lines 68–69) but says absolutely nothing about any letters of Peter.[68] Clement of Alexandria offers several allusions to 1 Peter and one direct quotation, and he also cites 1 John but no other Johannine letters, though when he refers to 1 John as the "larger epistle" (*Strom*. 2.15.66) he shows an acquaintance with at least one other. Jude seems to have been still less known. This little letter was used heavily but without acknowledgment by the author of 2 Peter (cf. 2 Pet. 2:1–18 and Jude 4—16), writing around 140(?). Otherwise, Jude is attested only late in the second century by Clement of Alexandria (Eusebius, *H.E.* 6.14.1), Tertullian (*De cultu feminarum* 1.3) and the Muratorian list (line 68), but the geographical diversity of these witnesses suggests that Jude must have had some broad currency in the preceding period. For the remaining catholic epistles—James, 3 John, and 2 Peter—there is simply no evidence for their use in the second century. They came into consideration as authoritative documents only later, and then with difficulty.

But just as some writings which were eventually to become part of the canon had not gained much, if any, notice by the end of the second century, other Christian writings enjoyed a large measure of early popularity but ultimately failed to gain canonical standing.

1 Clement, a letter from the Roman church to the Corinthian church written late in the first century, was widely known and valued in the second century and later. Irenaeus spoke of its author as one who "had seen the blessed apostles and had been conversant with them," and who therefore could be said "to have the preaching of the apostles still echoing in his ears and their traditions before his eyes" (*A.H.* 3.3.3). Hence, Irenaeus considered the letter a faithful source of apostolic teaching. The letter was also esteemed by Clement of Alexandria, who even calls it "a writing of the apostle Clement" (*Strom*. 4.17). Much later Eusebius confirms the popularity of *1 Clement* by remarking that "this letter was publicly read in the common assembly in many churches in the old days and in our own time" (*H.E.* 3.16).

The *Epistle of Barnabas* also acquired an early authority, especially

---

68. P. Katz, "The Johannine Epistles in the Muratorian Canon," *JTS* 8 (1957): 273–74, conjectured that the Greek original mentioned all three Johannine letters but that this is obscured in the Latin translation.

in churches of the east. Clement of Alexandria regarded it as a letter of the apostle Barnabas (*Strom*. 2.6; 7.5) and apparently discussed it in his *Hypotyposeis*, a fragmentarily preserved commentary on various writings, including some of the catholic epistles (Eusebius, *HE*. 6.14.1). The early popularity of *Barnabas* was sustained long enough for it to appear in some eastern canon lists from the fourth century.

The Shepherd of Hermas, an apocalypse composed in Rome about the middle of the second century, rapidly gained respect as authoritative scripture by reason of its claim to be an inspired revelation.[69] It was acknowledged without reservation as scripture by Irenaeus (*A.H.* 4.20.2; cf. Eusebius, *H.E.* 5.8.7), Clement of Alexandria (*Strom*. 1.17.29; 2.1.9,12) and Tertullian (*De oratione* 16). About this work the Muratorian list comments that since *The Shepherd* was composed recently, "it ought indeed to be read, but it cannot be read publicly in the church to the people either among the prophets, whose number is settled, or among the apostles to the end of time" (lines 77–80). Although *The Shepherd* is here excluded from the lectionary, its popularity is conceded. The appeal of this writing consisted especially in its teaching of the possibility of repentance after baptism, a relatively lenient position which was appreciated by many in the second and third centuries, though for the same reason Christians of a more rigorist stripe found *The Shepherd* objectionable.

The *Apocalypse of Peter* was also used as Christian scripture in this period. Clement of Alexandria commented on it in his *Hypotyposeis* (Eusebius, *H.E.* 6.14.1), and in the Muratorian list it is mentioned with approval along with Revelation, though it is also noted that "some of our people do not want it to be read in the church" (lines 72–73). But it found its way into several later eastern lists of authoritative books and seems to have been current mainly in the eastern churches.

Without discussing several other documents which had some early currency as scripture (*The Teaching of the Twelve Apostles, The Gospel of the Hebrews, Acts* of various apostles, etc.),[70] it is clear that a very large number of early Christian writings were valued as authoritative by the end of the second century. Among these the best known and most broadly used were our four Gospels and the letters of Paul, and the formation of these two collections was a large step toward the formation of a canon of Christian scripture. Yet plainly no such canon

69. See the remarks on the history *The Shepherd* by H. Chadwick, "The New Edition of Hermas," *JTS* 8 (1957): 274–80

70. For evidence on the knowledge and use of these documents in the ancient church, see the discussions in Hennecke and Schneemelcher, *NT Apocrypha*, 2 vols.

existed by the end of the second century, for beyond these basic collections there was wide variation in other writings similarly valued. Only Acts, 1 Peter, and 1 John had gained a really firm foothold. Both the idea and the shape of a Christian canon remained indeterminate.

THE THIRD AND FOURTH CENTURIES

The evidence for the history of the canon in the third century is slim but fascinating. A major figure for the first half of the third century is Origen of Alexandria (185–254), the greatest scripture scholar of the ancient church. Origen neither knew nor developed a formal list of authoritative Christian scriptures,[71] but he traveled widely and was conversant with the usages of many churches. In his profuse writings he often commented about various pieces of early Christian literature and offered his reasoned judgments about their authority. Most of these comments were summarized by Eusebius in a lengthy section of his *Ecclesiastical History* (*H.E.* 6.25.1–14), which provides a good index of Origen's views.[72] Origen gave full acknowledgment to only four Gospels, Matthew, Mark, Luke, and John, "which alone are unquestionable in the church of God under heaven" (*H.E.* 6.25.4). He also accepted the letters of Paul (*H.E.* 6.25.7). Further, Peter "has left one acknowledged letter." Origen was aware also of a second letter ascribed to Peter but noted that "it is doubted." Origen accepted Revelation and 1 John and set them down to the author of the fourth Gospel. He knew also of 2 and 3 John but observed that "not all say that these are genuine" (*H.E.* 6.25.10). His comments about Hebrews are especially interesting (*H.E.* 6.25.11–14). Observing that its literary style is not Paul's, Origen doubted whether Paul wrote it, but this did not compromise his admiration for Hebrews. He admitted that many assumed its Pauline authorship, while others attributed it to Clement of Rome and still others ascribed it to Luke, but Origen himself took an agnostic stance: "Who wrote the epistle, in truth only God knows." Among other writings known and used by Origen were Acts, James, Jude, *Barnabas*, *The Shepherd*, *Acts of Paul*, *Teaching of the Twelve Apostles*, and *1 Clement*. Clearly, Origen drew no definite or narrow limits on the literature which might count as authoritative in the church. Even when he appears to do so—as for example with the four Gospels—his usage is not absolutely strict, for he quotes numerous tra-

71. R. P. C. Hanson, *Origen's Doctrine of Tradition* (London: SPCK, 1954), 133–45.
72. For a fuller review of Origen's judgments, see ibid., 127–56, and J. Ruwet, "Les 'antilegomena' dans les œvres d'Origène," *Bib* 23 (1942): 18–42.

ditions from unknown sources and also put some stock in the *Gospel of Peter* and the *Gospel of the Hebrews*. On the whole, then, Origen symptomizes a state of affairs that was still rather fluid, though slightly more developed than in the time of his predecessor, Clement.

Evidence about usages in the west in the first part of the third century can be gleaned from Origen's near contemporary, Hippolytus (170–235), a presbyter in the Roman church. He employed as scripture the four Gospels, Paul's letters (excluding Hebrews), Acts, 1 Peter, 1 and 2 John, and Revelation. Hippolytus also valued various other documents, including Hebrews, *The Shepherd, Apocalypse of Peter, Acts of Paul,* James, Jude, and 2 Peter (of this last Hippolytus is the first writer to show any knowledge at all). But Hippolytus's chief importance for the history of the canon lies in his authorship of a treatise entitled "Points Against Gaius." This work was occasioned by the learned Roman churchman Gaius, who early in the third century composed a "Dialogue with Proclus" in order to refute Montanist teachings, of which Proclus was a leading spokesman. Gaius's "Dialogue with Proclus" consisted at least in part of a close literary and historical criticism of the Gospel of John and Revelation, on the basis of which Gaius denied the authenticity and authority of both documents. This repudiation of John and Revelation was of a piece with Gaius's attack on Montanism, for the Montanists appealed to both writings in support of their own claims; but it shows nevertheless that neither John nor Revelation was so securely fixed in the church's esteem even in the early third century that it could not be rejected by an orthodox thinker.[73] In his "Points Against Gaius," Hippolytus set about to neutralize Gaius's criticisms of these books, and in this he succeeded well enough that after his time John and Revelation were firmly held as authoritative in the west.

In the east, however, the authority of Revelation remained a point of contention. While Origen had apparently accepted the book (though he interpreted it allegorically), it came increasingly into question later on, mainly under the influence of Dionysius, bishop of Alexandria, about the middle of the third century. His concern with Revelation was prompted by Nepos of Arsinoe, who wrote a treatise entitled "Refutation of the Allegorists" in which he rejected the allegorical interpretation of Revelation and insisted on a literal reading in support of millennial ideas. Dionysius responded with a work named "On

73. The most comprehensive and instructive study of this dispute is J. D. Smith, "Gaius and the Controversy Over the Johannine Literature," (Ph.D. diss., Yale Univ., 1979).

Promises," and from this Eusebius (*H.E.* 7.25) has preserved some interesting excerpts.[74] Here Dionysius remarked that he would not himself reject the book Revelation "since many brethren hold it in esteem," but he confessed that Revelation was incomprehensible to him (*H.E.* 7.25.4–5). He proceeded to make many acute observations about the language, style, and thought of Revelation which decisively differentiate it from the Gospel of John and 1 John (*H.E.* 7.25.17–27). Since these insights compelled Dionysius to deny that Revelation was written by the same author, he disputed its apostolic origin. Dionysius's hesitancy toward Revelation was not merely or even mainly a result of his doubts about authorship. Rather, he was troubled by the use being made of it by millennialists who gave the work a literal interpretation and conjured up expectations about an earthly kingdom (*H.E.* 7.25.1–5). Thus, the basic considerations were doctrinal and hermeneutical, and the question of authorship was ancillary to these. In any case, Dionysius's criticisms eroded what standing Revelation had gained in the east, and later on, eastern Christian writers generally rejected it.

In the west the fate of Hebrews was in some respects comparable. It was more or less consistently neglected there until the late fourth century.[75] This was due in no small part to the very teaching of this document which had appealed to Tertullian and other moral rigorists such as the Montanists: namely, that sins committed after baptism could not be forgiven (6:4–8; 10:26–31; 12:14–17). This was completely out of step with the rapidly developing penitential ideas and practices of the western church. In addition, the west had well-founded doubts about the authorship of Hebrews and lacked any inclination to attribute it to Paul, as the east had done. As in the case of Revelation in the east, it was perhaps first of all the problem of content, not authorship, which made Hebrews suspect. Theological reservations drew questions of authorship in their wake. As a result, Hebrews was not valued as scripture in the western church throughout the third century, and in the early fourth century Eusebius could remark (*H.E.* 6.20.30) that "even to this day among the Romans there are some who do not consider it to be the apostle's." It was only late in the fourth century, in fact, that Hebrews began to enjoy general use and authority in the west.

74. Cf. Stonehouse, *Apocalypse,* 123–28.
75. It is not mentioned in the Muratorian list, and although Irenaeus may have used it (Eusebius, *H.E.* 5.26), neither he nor Hippolytus seems to have regarded it as Pauline. Cyprian of Carthage shows no knowledge of it at all.

It will have become obvious that one of the most important resources for recovering the history of the canon is the *Ecclesiastical
History* of Eusebius, bishop of Caesarea in Palestine (ca. 265–340). In
composing this work, completed about 325, Eusebius inquired into
earlier usages of Christian writings in the church and recorded many
useful bits of evidence on this topic. But here it is a question of Eusebius's statements about the status of various documents in the churches
of his own day, for which he is also a valuable witness. He provides a
threefold classification of the writings (*H.E.* 3.25.1–7): "acknowledged
books" (*homologoumenoi*), "disputed books" (*antilegomenoi* and *no-
tha*), and heretical works.[76] In the category of "acknowledged books"—
that is, those received as authoritative scripture—Eusebius includes
the four Gospels, Acts, the letters of Paul (presumably including Hebrews), 1 John, and 1 Peter. He also allows that Revelation *may* be
placed in this group "if it seem desirable." In the larger category of
"disputed books" he places James, Jude, 2 Peter, 2 and 3 John, and
in addition, *Acts of Paul, The Shepherd* of Hermas, *Apocalypse of
Peter, Barnabas,* and *Teaching of the Twelve Apostles.* Then he adds,
rather remarkably, that Revelation *may* be classed among the disputed
books "if this view prevail," and furthermore that some would reckon
the *Gospel of the Hebrews* among the acknowledged books. Judging
from Eusebius's presentation, it seems that little development had
taken place during the third century: the writings placed in the "acknowledged" group are precisely those which had come to be generally
recognized by the end of the second century. Apart from 1 Peter and
1 John, the other "catholic epistles" had not gained general recognition
even by Eusebius's time[77]; and Revelation continued to be in an equiv-
ocal position (as did Hebrews in the west, but Eusebius reflects here
the eastern bias); and a large number of writings fall into the "disputed" category. Thus, the question of the scope of Christian scripture
was still a lively one with Eusebius.

Later in the fourth century, efforts began in earnest to draw up
definitive lists of Christian scripture. One of the earliest of these is
preserved in Codex Claromontanus, a bilingual Greek-Latin ms. of
the sixth century. The list it contains, however, is much earlier than

---

76. Most have supposed that Eusebius provides not three but four categories: acknowledged, disputed, spurious, and heretical. The analysis of the passage by E. Kalin, "Argument from Inspiration
in the Canonization of the New Testament" (Ph.D. diss., Harvard Univ., 1967), 141–55, shows that
for Eusebius "disputed" and "spurious" are synonymous, so that only three divisions are in view.
77. Though Eusebius is the first to speak of "the seven catholic epistles" (*H.E.* 2.23.25), he himself
makes no use of Jude, 2 Peter, or 2 or 3 John.

the ms. itself and was probably formulated in the east in the fourth century. This list specifies, in order, the four Gospels, ten letters of Paul, the seven catholic epistles, *Barnabas,* Revelation, Acts, *The Shepherd* of Hermas, the *Acts of Paul,* and the *Apocalypse of Peter.* The omission of Philippians and 1 and 2 Thessalonians from the letters of Paul is certainly accidental (perhaps this is true of Hebrews also), but the inclusion of the other documents is typical of the period.[78] It should be noted, however, that *Barnabas, The Shepherd,* the *Acts of Paul,* and the *Apocalypse of Peter* each has a scribal mark before it, which must indicate some hesitation about these items, if not in the original list, then by a later copyist. Nevertheless, the catalogue in Claromontanus offers thirty documents as comprising "the holy scriptures."

Another early list is the so-called Cheltenham canon, which probably originated about 360 in North Africa. It introduces the list of Christian scriptures with the statement: "As it is said in the Apocalypse of John, 'I saw twenty-four elders presenting their crowns before the throne' [Rev. 4:10], so our fathers approved that these books are canonical and that the men of old have said this." Thus, a collection of twenty-four writings is legitimized by an appeal both to an inspired statement of Revelation (allegorically interpreted) and to the authority of traditional usage. The list includes the four Gospels, thirteen letters of Paul, Acts, Revelation, three letters of John, and two of Peter. Here, too, there are interesting features. Hebrews, James, and Jude are omitted, and after the mention of three letters of John and again after the mention of two letters of Peter, there occurs the notation *una sola,* "one only." This suggests a decided preference for only 1 John and 1 Peter, and this is in line with the early tendency to grant full recognition to only these two documents among the catholic epistles.

An important document among fourth-century lists of Christian scriptures is the thirty-ninth Festal Letter of Athanasius, bishop of Alexandria, issued in 367. To regularize the usages of churches in Egypt and to disenfranchise heretical teachings supported from spurious documents, Athanasius set forth a list of those writings "handed on by tradition and believed to be divine" and "in which alone the godly doctrine is proclaimed." His is the first list to name as exclusively authoritative exactly the twenty-seven books which make up our NT. Athanasius was the first eastern Christian writer since Origen to rec-

---

78. Codex Sinaiticus (fourth century) includes both the *Epistle of Barnabas* and *The Shepherd* in its New Testament; Codex Alexandrinus (fifth century) includes *1 Clement* and *2 Clement.*

ognize Revelation, and in this his acquaintaince with western habits must have been influential.

Athanasius's definition of the canon for Egypt was not decisive for other regions of the eastern church.[79] The practice of Syrian Christianity, which was highly conservative, persisted on a different course. The popularity of Tatian's *Diatessaron* continued there during the fourth century, even when the separate Gospels were known. In addition to the Gospels, Syrian Christianity normally recognized only Acts and the letters of Paul, and nothing more. There was a growing tendency, probably under Alexandrian influence, to admit Hebrews among the letters of Paul, and for a while the pseudonymous *3 Corinthians* was also acknowledged, whereas the undoubtedly genuine Philemon was not recognized until quite late. None of the catholic epistles had any currency in the Syrian church until the late fourth and early fifth centuries, and then only James, 1 Peter, and 1 John secured any standing. The traditional Syrian preference for only the Gospels, Acts, and Paul's letters is still to be seen in Ephraem (d. 373), the *Doctrine of Addai* (350–400), a canon list of ca. 400, and Theodore, bishop of Mopsuestia (d. 428). The recognition of James, 1 Peter, and 1 John is attested by Chrysostom (fl. 380), the Syriac Peshitta list (ca. 410) and Theodoret (fl. 440). Thus, even into the early fifth century, the Syrian church typically admitted only twenty-two books.

The final resolution of the many variations we have noted began to take place in the late fourth century, primarily through the actions of ecclesiastical councils. One of the earliest conciliar pronouncements is associated with the Council of Laodicea, held in 363. It apparently specified as suitable for reading in the church "only the canonical books," of which twenty-six were enumerated. This list agrees with our NT except that it omits Revelation, which is probably due to the influence of Eusebius and Syrian tradition. Somewhat less certainty about the scope of the canon in the east is indicated by Amphilochus of Iconium (fl. 380), who included Hebrews in his list but noted that "some mistakenly reject it," and who observed that regarding the catholic epistles "some say seven, but others only three, one of James, one of Peter and one of John." As for Revelation, he noted that "some receive it, but the majority call in uncanonical."

In the west, two North African synods of the late fourth century

79. Athanasius's list was not altogether decisive even for Egypt, as shown by B. Ehrman, "The New Testament Canon of Didymus the Blind," *VC* 37 (1983): 1–21.

promulgated lists of authoritative books. The Council of Hippo (393) and the Council of Carthage (397) both named the twenty-seven books of our NT. But they still distinguished Hebrews from the letters of Paul, speaking first of "thirteen letters of the apostle Paul" and then adding, "of the same, one to the Hebrews."[80] The way for the admission of Hebrews in the west had been paved by Hilary of Poitiers (d. 366), Ambrose of Milan (d. 397), and Rufinus of Aquileia (d. 410), all of whom used it as canonical while nevertheless regarding it as anonymous. Clearly, the western recognition of Hebrews did not depend on a persuasion of Pauline authorship. But with the Council of Carthage in 418, Hebrews was finally fully integrated into the Pauline collection; and its approval by Jerome, who was much under eastern influence, insured that it would no longer be challenged in the west.

In sum, the writings which found the least and most hesitating recognition in the ancient church were James, Jude, 2 Peter, and 2 and 3 John. Their status was almost everywhere questionable before the middle of the fourth century. But also the acknowledgment of Hebrews and Revelation was fitful and uneven, and the acceptance of Hebrews in the west and of Revelation in the east did not become firm until the late fourth century. A broad uniformity of usage which closely approximates our NT cannot therefore be dated before the close of the fourth century, and even then the Syrian church lagged behind. It needs to be emphasized, however, that this emergent uniformity was fundamentally de facto, for no ecumenical authority of the ancient church ever rendered a formal decision for the church at large as to the exact contents of Christian scripture.

80. On the varying regard for Hebrews and its placement relative to the Pauline letters, see W. H. P. Hatch, "The Position of Hebrews in the Canon of the New Testament," *HTR* 29 (1936): 133–51. A concise summary of the evidence is given by B. Metzger, *Textual Commentary*, 661–62.

III

Factors in
the Formation of the Canon

A complex interplay of ideas, circumstances, and historical forces conspired to create the concept of a canon of Christian scriptures, to influence the pace and direction of its development, and to determine its contents. Apart from these, the existence and the character of the NT are hardly to be understood.

INTRINSIC FACTORS

Christianity did not begin as a scriptural religion. The faith of the earliest Christians was evoked by and focused on a person, Jesus of Nazareth, and he was apprehended not in written texts but in the preaching about him as the crucified and risen Messiah, and in the charismatic life of the Christian community. The immediacy of Christian experience and the fervor of its eschatological hopes made superfluous even the composition of Christian writings, and there is no intimation at all that the early church entertained the idea of Christian scriptures, much less a collection of them. Therefore, the NT as we think of it was utterly remote from the minds of the first generations of Christian believers.

Of course, almost from the start Christianity had called into service the scriptures of Judaism, interpreting them as the prophetic witness of which the Christian faith was the fulfillment.[1] Even so, these Jewish scriptures only supported and confirmed the Christian message; they did not constitute its basis or give it adequate expression. Thus, the Christian use of Jewish scriptures did not mean that Christianity was

---

1. Among many treatments, see esp. C. H. Dodd, *According to the Scriptures: The Sub-Structure of New Testament Theology* (London: James Nisbet & Co., 1952); B. Lindars, *New Testament Apologetic: The Doctrinal Significance of the Old Testament Quotations* (London: SCM Press, 1961); D. M. Smith, "The Use of the Old Testament in the New," in *The Use of Old Testament in the New and Other Essays: Studies in Honor of W. F. Stinespring*, ed. J. M. Efird (Durham, N.C.: Duke Univ. Press, 1972), 3–65.

or would become a scriptural religion after the pattern of Judaism, nor that there should also be distinctively Christian scriptures. Just as little did it suggest the notion of a canon of Christian writings, because the scriptures of Judaism themselves had not yet been shaped into a definitive and closed collection.[2] The appeal to Jewish scriptures, though very important in early Christianity, could not finally suffice for Christian needs. The legitimacy of the Christian interpretation of these Jewish writings was challenged and repudiated by Judaism itself and could not be taken for granted even within the church.[3] Moreover, as its missionary efforts carried it well beyond the confines of Judaism, Christianity found its most responsive constituency among Gentiles who were often ill acquainted with the Jewish scriptures and did not immediately presume their authority. In this context it was difficult to present Christian teachings on the basis of Jewish scriptures alone, and appeals to specifically Christian writings were more and more needed.

Since the Christian community lodged revelatory and redemptive meaning in a particular historical person and a specific historical period, it was essential that the church should always hark back to the figure of Jesus and the events of his life, death, and resurrection. This indispensable recourse was provided at first through the direct witness of apostolic preaching and a lively oral tradition. But the passage of time, the demise of the apostles, and the dissipation of oral tradition both led to the composition of Christian writings and elevated their importance as means of sustaining the church's relationship to the decisive events of its origins. After a point, however, this relationship could be maintained reliably only through written testimony which stood relatively close to the period of revelation.[4] To this extent it may be said that the valuation of certain writings and even the eventual development of a canon of authoritative writings were tendencies inherent in the very nature of Christianity.

Thus, the scriptures of Judaism and literature produced within Christianity were read together in the context of Christian worship. This did not presume or imply that Christian writings possessed the inspired and oracular character of the Jewish scriptures, but the as-

2. A. C. Sundberg, Jr., *The Old Testament of the Early Church*, HTS 20 (Cambridge: Harvard Univ. Press, 1964), summarized in "The Old Testament of the Early Church," *HTR* 51 (1958): 205–26. Cf. Sundberg, "The 'Old Testament': A Christian Canon," *CBQ* 30 (1968): 143–65.
3. See the discussion by Campenhausen, *Formation*, 21–102.
4. W. G. Kümmel, "Notwendigkeit und Grenze des neutestamentlichen Kanons," *ZTK* 47 (1950): 277–313.

sociated use of these different bodies of religious literature led over time to a scriptural estimate of Christian writings and to their grouping as a counterpart to Jewish scripture. Eventually it promoted the belief that these two groups of scriptures, however different in origin and content, shared the same authoritative value for Christian faith. But these were gradual perceptions, and they took effect only in conjunction with other influences on the formation of the NT canon.

EXTRINSIC FACTORS

Among the varied forces which impinged on the history of the canon, a special significance has usually been found in the theological controversies which engaged the church during the second century—namely, Marcionism, Gnosticism, and Montanism. These need to be carefully assessed.

Marcionism

Marcion was one of the most imposing figures of second-century Christianity.[5] A native of Sinope, a city of northern Asia Minor on the coast of the Black Sea, and the son of a well-to-do shipowner, Marcion came to Rome about 140 and there became a teacher and benefactor of the Roman church. When about 144 a dispute arose over Marcion's teaching, he and his followers separated from the Roman church and established a vigorous movement based on his own particular conception of Christianity. Marcion taught that Christianity comprised an utterly new and unparalleled revelation given by a different and higher God than the God of Israel. The Christian God, he maintained, was a god of love and mercy, whereas the God of Israel was a god of justice and vengeance. As the former had nothing to do with the latter, so also Christianity had nothing to do with Judaism, and therefore the scripture of Judaism had no place in the church. Marcion located the true Christian teaching in the letters of Paul and the Gospel of Luke, believing that Paul alone was a faithful apostle of Christ and had alone grasped the essence of the new revelation. He carefully edited these writings, removing supposedly Jewish adulterations, and set them up as the exclusive resource and standard of Christian belief. Thus, the first known canon of Christian writings was the creation of Marcion, and it was characterized by a twofold structure: Gospel literature and

5. In addition to Harnack's *Marcion*, see also E. C. Blackman, *Marcion and His Influence* (London: SPCK, 1948); the recent appraisals by B. Aland, "Marcion: Versuch einer neuen Interpretation," *ZTK* 70 (1973): 420–47; and D. Balas, "Marcion Revisited: A Post-Harnack Perspective," in *Texts and Testaments*, 95–108.

apostolic letters. Although Marcion and his teaching were quickly repudiated as heterodox, historians of the canon have often supposed
that Marcion had a decisive impact on the formation of the NT. In
particular, it has been argued that Marcion was the first to conceive
and develop the idea of a collection of authoritative Christian writings
and that the catholic NT came into being as a reaction to Marcion and
in imitation of him: "The NT is an anti-marcionite creation on a marcionite basis."[6] Is this high estimate of Marcion's role warranted?

The chronological priority of Marcion's canon is, of course, indisputable: nothing like this precedes him. But the chronological prec-
edence of Marcion's canon has to be distinguished from the question
of its influence on the church. This influence has been seen in several
ways: Marcion's canon is thought to have posed an inescapable necessity for the church to counter him by fixing a canon of its own; Marcion
supposedly provided the structural principle of Gospel-Apostle on which
the catholic canon is built; Marcion's use of Paul's letters is seen as
the cause of the prominence of Paul in the canon of the church (which
could not afford to honor Paul less than Marcion had); and the church
was compelled to compensate Marcion's one-sided emphasis on Paul
by incorporating a larger and more diverse number of apostolic writings. But in none of these particulars is it clear that Marcion's canon
furnished the cause or even had any influence. The fixation of a canon
by Marcion did not in fact lead to an immediate or concerted effort in
the church to delimit its own authoritative literature, and the number
of writings valued continued for a long time to be large and fluid.
Further, although the literary conjunction of Gospel and apostle is
first clearly seen with Marcion, the dual appeal to "the Lord and the
apostles" was current well before his time and had already found
expression in the high valuation of the traditions about Jesus and in
the collection of Paul's letters. Also, the prominence of Paul's letters
in the catholic canon probably owed little or nothing to Marcion; the
fact that they had been available in a widely known collection before
Marcion, their abundance and indisputable authenticity, and the relative paucity of other apostolic writings insured that Paul's letters
would be esteemed independently of Marcion.[7] And finally, the fact
that the catholic canon came to have broader scope than Marcion's is
no more adequately explained as a reaction against Marcion than as a

6. Harnack, *Marcion*, 444*, cf. 210–15, and *Origin of the NT*, 30–35, 57–60. Similar conclusions
are reached by Knox, *Marcion*, 19–38; and Campenhausen, *Formation*, 148–63, and "Marcion et
les origines du canon néotestamentaire," *RHPR* 46 (1966):213–26.
7. See above, 41–43.

result of historic usages in the church. Thus, the evidence for Marcion's influence on the history of the canon, so far as it is merely circumstantial, is not very strong. But evidence of a documentary sort has also been suggested. This consists of the so-called Marcionite prologues to the Pauline letters and the so-called anti-Marcionite prologues to the Gospels.

The old prologues to Paul's letters have commonly been regarded as Marcionite on the grounds that they presuppose Marcion's arrangement of the letters and reflect Marcionite theological ideas. Their presence in a number of Vulgate mss. of the NT is often alleged as proof of Marcion's impact on the catholic canon.[8] But this argument has become increasingly tenuous. Marcion was not the only one in the ancient church who had Paul's letters in this arrangement, and the peculiarity of this arrangement, which consists chiefly in putting Galatians first, is more likely to result from an effort to offer the letters in chronological order than from a dogmatic bias of Marcion in favor of Galatians.[9] In that case, a major argument for a Marcionite origin of the prologues is lost. In terms of their ideology, the prologues contain elements which seem typically Marcionite but nothing that is definitely Marcionite. That they call Paul "the apostle" (as if he were the only one) is due simply to the fact that the prologues are concerned only with his letters. And the stereotyped references in the prologues to Paul's opponents as Judaizing teachers do not necessarily betray a Marcionite mind-set; they may just as well be understood as compositions of a catholic writer who assuredly had an anti-Judaizing attitude but no Marcionite sympathies.[10] Hence, it is most unlikely that these prologues are Marcionite products or signify Marcion's influence on the shaping of the canon.

The so-called anti-Marcionite prologues to the Gospels have sometimes been regarded as early compositions aimed to counter Marcion and thus also as evidence that the church fashioned its four-Gospel collection in direct opposition to him.[11] But this view has been dis-

---

8. The Marcionite character of these prologues was independently alleged by D. de Bruyne, "Prologues bibliques d'origin marcionite," *RBen* 24 (1907): 1–14, and P. Corssen, "Zur Überlieferungsgeschichte des Römerbriefes," *ZNW* 10 (1909): 1–45, esp. 36–45. The case has been refined and restated by K. Th. Schäfer, "Marcion und die ältesten Prologe zu den Paulusbriefen," in *Kyriakon: Festschrift J. Quasten*, ed. P. Granfeld and J. A. Jungmann (Münster: Aschendorff, 1973), 135–50.

9. H. J. Frede, "Altlateinischen Paulus-Handschriften," in *Vetus Latina. Aus der Geschichte der lateinischen Bibel* 4 (Freiburg: Herder, 1964), 171–78, and "Die Ordnung der Paulusbriefe," 295–96.

10. N. A. Dahl, "The Origin of the Earliest Prologues," 233–77.

11. D. de Bruyne, "Les plus anciens prologues latines des Evangiles," *RBen* 40 (1928): 193–214; and Adolf von Harnack, "Die ältesten Evangelien-Prologe und die Bildung des Neuen Testaments," SPAW.PH 24 (1928): 322–41.

credited in recent years. Unlike the prologues to Paul's letters, these Gospel prologues do not constitute a unified set but were composed at different times and from different perspectives; they do not collectively possess a specifically anti-Marcionite intention; and it now appears that these prologues derive not from the second but from the fourth century, by which time the controversy with Marcion had only antiquarian interest.[12] Therefore, the alleged documentary evidence for Marcion's influence actually contributes nothing to the circumstantial evidence.

There is not yet any unanimity among modern scholars about the importance of Marcion for the canon of the NT. Instead of the view that he originated the idea of a canon and provided both the stimulus and structure of the catholic canon, some have expressed the more moderate opinion that, though Marcion was not a crucial factor, he nevertheless hastened the development of the canon, causing the church to do more quickly what it would eventually have done anyway.[13] But even this modest tribute may not be justified, since it is not possible to know whether the process of canon formation would have moved at a different pace had there never been a Marcion. In the absence of stronger evidence, it is gratuitous to see in Marcion a decisive factor in the history of the NT canon.

Gnosticism

Beyond Marcion, almost throughout the second century the church was engaged in controversy with gnostic types of Christianity and their illustrious teachers. Although gnostic varieties of Christianity were almost as old as Christianity itself, they were progressively disenfranchised and finally repudiated as Christianity became consolidated into an "orthodox" theology. It has often been supposed that the NT canon was forged as a weapon in the conflict with Gnosticism. Here two considerations come into play. First, many writings were produced and valued in gnostic circles during the second century, so that the literary resources of gnostic Christianity were more abundant than those of more conventional churches.[14] Second, it was characteristic of gnostic Christians to support their teachings by appeals to special,

---

12. J. Regul, "Die antimarcionitischen Evangelienprologe," in *Vetus Latina. Aus der Geschichte der lateinischen Bibel* 6 (Freiburg: Herder, 1969).

13. E.g., Blackman, *Marcion*, 39; F. V. Filson, *Which Books Belong to the Bible?* (Philadelphia: Westminster Press, 1957), 120; Kümmel, "Notwendigkeit und Grenze," 238.

14. For gnostic Christian literature, see Hennecke and Schneemelcher, *NT Apocrypha*, 1:231–62, and J. M. Robinson, *The Nag Hammadi Library* (New York: Harper & Row, 1977).

esoteric traditions not accessible outside gnostic communities. It may be conjectured, then, that the formation of the canon was a calculated effort to oppose these tendencies, on the one hand by rejecting gnostic literature, and on the other hand by affirming the sole authority of broadly recognized and publicly accessible documents embodying apostolic and catholic teaching. In fact, anti-heretical writers of the late second century do make this sort of appeal to Christian scriptures.[15]

As useful as this appeal may have been, it does not show that the canon was created with this end in view, or even that it was entirely serviceable for this purpose. While gnostic groups did produce their own literature, they also made full and free use of those early Christian writings which were in general esteem. The difference between gnostic Christianity and the church at large lay less in appeals to different writings that in different hermeneutical approaches to much of the same literature.[16] For this reason the anti-heretical writers were seldom in a position to reject the authority of the writings used by the gnostics but were constrained instead to urge an alternative interpretation of it. Consequently, the formation of the canon could not by itself have been an effective anti-gnostic strategem. But having said this, it also has to be noted that exegetical recourse to Christian writings in support of theological argument was early practiced by gnostic Christians and possibly even originated with them.[17] This gave positive stimulus to the valuation of this literature and so at least indirectly to the process of shaping the canon.

Montanism

Along with Marcion and the Gnostics, Montanism has also been seen as a provocation to the formation of the NT.[18] This movement flowered in Asia Minor soon after the middle of the second century under the leadership of Montanus, who claimed that the Paraclete promised by Jesus in the Gospel of John (14:16, 26; 15:26; 16:12–15) had now come and, through Montanus himself and his prophetic as-

15. Irenaeus is an excellent example. See Campenhausen, *Formation*, 185–209.
16. Grant, *Formation*, 121–30; H. E. W. Turner, *The Pattern of Christian Truth: A Study in the Relations between Orthodoxy and Heresy in the Early Church* (London: Mowbray, 1954), 180–86, 232–38; Hanson, *Tradition in the Early Church*, 197–201. For the nature and results of gnostic exegesis, see esp. the studies of E. Pagels, *The Johannine Gospel* and *The Gnostic Paul* (Philadelphia: Fortress Press, 1975). But for the gnostic interpretation of Paul, see the careful discussion in Rensberger, "As the Apostle Teaches," 134–49, 218–63.
17. Grant, *Formation*, 121–24.
18. See, among others, Harnack, *Origin of the NT*, 34–39; Campenhausen, *Formation*, 210–42; H. Paulsen, "Die Bedeutung des Montanismus für die Herausbildung des Kanons," *VC* 32 (1978): 19–52.

sociates, was offering new and final revelations to the church. Speaking with charismatic authority, the movement announced that the last days were at hand and insisted on a stringent morality in view of impending judgment and salvation. Such apocalyptic fervor and moral rigorism had been typical features of primitive Christianity, but the church of the late second century had developed well beyond these aboriginal elements and mounted an energetic campaign to discredit Montanist teachings. This was no easy task, since Montanism claimed continuities with the earliest church, drew upon early Christian writings, declared no new doctrines, and proved to be widely popular not only in Asia Minor but also in Rome and North Africa. The effect of Montanism on the history of the canon is usually lodged in two points. First, since the prophetic oracles of Montanus and his followers were sometimes compiled in written form and cited as authoritative, the church had to disclaim these by specifying which writings did have authoritative value. Second, and more important, because Montanism asserted new and continuing revelation, the church was led to insist that inspired revelation was confined to an age now past—the age of Christ and the apostles—and that only such teachings as derived from that time had binding force. By calling forth this reaction, Montanism supposedly precipitated the conception of a *closed* canon to which nothing new is admissible. Thus, just as Marcion is often credited with conceiving the idea of a canon and forcing the church, in reaction to him, to enlarge the scope of its authoritative scripture, so Montanism can be viewed as later furnishing the opposite impetus to limit the scope of authoritative writings.

This assessment of Montanism's importance is very doubtful. If the Montanists composed written collections of their oracles and perhaps some other works, it does not seem that they appealed to these as scripture or thought of them as supplementing Christian writings which had a general and longstanding authority.[19] Certainly, the Montanists did not reject writings which were generally recognized but freely employed them to support Montanist ideas.[20] Therefore, Montanism cannot be said to have provoked an emphasis on the normative character of Christian writings (as opposed to new prophetic revelations). In fact, arguments about scripture and arguments from scripture played a remarkably small role in the whole conflict, whose issues seem not

19. Campenhausen, *Formation*, 227; F. E. Vokes, "The Use of Scripture in the Montanist Controversy," *StEv* 5 (1968): 317–20.
20. Paulsen, "Die Bedeutung des Montanismus," 22–32.

to have been focused in the problems of written versus unwritten authority or of old versus new writings. Furthermore, the church did not as a result of the Montanist crisis confine inspired revelation to the apostolic past. Both during and after the heyday of Montanism, the activity of the Spirit in the church was fully affirmed, and even anti-Montanist writers laid positive emphasis on the prophetic charisma and so did not think that ecstatic prophecy and authoritative writings were mutually exclusive sources of Christian teaching.[21] For these reasons Montanism cannot be deemed a crucial factor in the shaping of the canon. It highlighted some related issues, such as the nature and meaning of historical tradition, the relation of past and present revelation, the authority of certain documents (John, Revelation), and the prerogative of their interpretation.[22] But there is no good evidence that it called forth the idea of a closed canon of scripture.

Even though a special and determinative impact on the formation of the NT canon cannot be assigned to any one of these second-century controversies, their collective importance ought not to be underestimated. The diverse conceptions of Christianity exemplified in these movements required their opponents to define more exactly the substance of the Christian confession, to specify its proper resources, and to safeguard it against criticism and deviation. The tendency to ascribe authority to certain traditional documents and to make argumentative theological appeals to them was an important part of this effort. But this was not effective apart from the concurrent tendencies to formulate Christian belief in concise and summary form and to lodge the prerogative of teaching and interpretation with authoritative ecclesiastical officers.[23]

Other Factors

Many other factors also played a role in shaping the NT, though it is not easy to gauge their importance. So, for example, the *opinions of respected theologians* (whether or not they happened also to be bishops) were often widely influential.[24] Striking examples of this can be seen in such figures as Origen and Athanasius in the eastern church

21. Kalin, "Argument from Inspiration," and J. L. Ash, "The Decline of Ecstatic Prophecy in the Early Church," *TS* 37 (1976): 227–52.

22. Paulsen, "Die Bedeutung des Montanismus," 32–52.

23. The formation of the canon as such could not be a decisive response, since the most pressing question was not which writings were authoritative but, rather, how they should be interpreted.

24. K. Aland, *The Problem of the New Testament Canon* (London: Mowbray, 1962), 20–22.

and Jerome and Augustine in the western. For the fortunes of some individual writings (e.g., Revelation, Hebrews) the judgments of such thinkers were crucial, even though in the whole process of canon formation the ideas of individual theologians were not conclusive. Again, the history of the canon, like the history of the ancient church generally, shows the effects of the *political rivalries, cultural differences, and theological orientations* of the great centers of ecclesiastical influence: above all, Rome, Alexandria, and Antioch.[25] The theological conservatism of Antiochene Christianity and its bent toward a literal-historical type of interpretation are symptomized in the narrow, highly traditional collection of scriptures which persisted for so long in that region. Conversely, the open and speculative cast of Alexandrian Christianity with its commitment to allegorical exegesis is reflected in the rich trove of early Christian literature valued in Egypt. As in doctrinal, so also in canonical matters Rome generally charted a pragmatic middle course between these extremes. Further, some impetus to the production of lists discriminating between authoritative and nonauthoritative writings is perhaps also to be located in the church's *experience of persecution,* which often involved the proscription, requisition, and destruction of Christian scriptures by local or provincial authorities.[26] Such situations may have prompted the church toward decisions about which books were to be held sacred and retained from the authorities and which ones might be surrendered without blame. And, so far as canonization is understood strictly as the determination of a fixed and closed list of authoritative scriptures, *official ecclesiastical decisions* rendered by bishops or councils must be given their due.[27] We do not know of any such decisions prior to the last half of the fourth century, by which time many documents had been in such long and wide use that an official decision could only confirm standing practice. But this was not true of all documents which found a place in the canon, and ecclesiastical pronouncements were instrumental in bringing some writings to full canonical recognition—for example, Hebrews in the west and Revelation in the east. The judgments of ecclesiastical authorities were more important than this, however, because they had the effect of concluding discussion about the

---

25. See esp. H. Lietzmann, "Wie wurden die Bücher des Neuen Testament Heilige Schrift?" in *Kleine Schriften* 2, "Studien zum Neuen Testament," ed. K. Aland (=TU 68; Berlin: Akademie-Verlag, 1958), 15–98.

26. Cf. W. R. Farmer, *Jesus and the Gospel: Tradition, Scripture, and Canon* (Philadelphia: Fortress Press, 1982), 177–259. He, however, goes too far in finding here the basic motive for the formation and substance of the canon.

27. Sundberg, "Toward a Revised History," 461.

authority of individual writings and of finalizing the scope of the canon. In this sense it is entirely legitimate to say that as a closed collection, to which nothing may be added and from which nothing may be deleted, the NT canon is contingent on official decisions of the church. Finally, the history of the canon cannot be completely separated even from so ordinary a matter as *the history of book manufacture* in the ancient world.[28] Virtually from the beginning, Christianity made use of the codex (or leaf book) rather than the roll (or scroll). But the codex was in the first century something of an innovation and not yet well developed, so that its capacity was small and long remained quite limited. So long as this was true, a given codex could not contain more than a few writings, perhaps several Gospels or the letters of Paul or other small collections. It was not until the fourth century that the technology of bookmaking produced codices capable of containing the whole of the Christian scriptures. It is probably not mere coincidence, therefore, that the NT acquired a relatively fixed content only when codices became large enough to permit these various writings to be transcribed in a single book. This merely technical factor both contributed to the stability of the canon and for the first time gave tangible form to the collection and differentiation of these writings from all others.

CRITERIA OF CANONICITY

If the formation of the NT canon was indebted to many contingent historical factors, it was not a thoroughly random process. The church also engaged in a reflective evaluation of its literary and theological heritage, and in setting apart certain documents as specially authoritative, it appealed to certain principles. Because these principles were not invoked with great rigor or consistency, it is difficult to assess their actual effects on the history of the canon, and there is disagreement today about the meaning or importance of the so-called criteria of canonicity.[29] The criteria that figured most prominently in the thinking

28. On this, see now esp. C. H. Roberts and T. C. Skeat, *The Birth of the Codex* (New York and London: Oxford Univ. Press, 1983), and E. G. Turner, *The Typology of the Early Codex* (Philadelphia: Univ. of Pennsylvania Press, 1977).

29. So, e.g., E. Flesseman van Leer ("Prinzipien der Sammlung und Ausscheidung bei der Bildung des Kanons," *ZTK* [1964]: 404–20) specifies apostolicity and inspiration as the decisive criteria in the west and east, respectively; Campenhausen (*Formation*, 330) thinks the main principle was chronological, so that authoritative writings must derive from the period closest to Christ, authorship playing no important role; K. Aland (*Problem of the NT Canon*, 14–15) suggests that in the history of the canon "one can speak only of the principle of having no principles." The most thorough study of the criteria of canonicity is K.-H. Ohlig, *Die theologische Begründung des neutestamentlichen Kanons in der alten Kirche*, KBANT (Düsseldorf: Patmos-Verlag, 1972); for a summary, cf. his *Woher nimmt die Bibel ihre Autorität?* (Düsseldorf: Patmos-Verlag, 1970), 59–91.

of the church were apostolicity, catholicity, orthodoxy, and established usage.

Apostolicity

In popular Christian thinking, the apostolicity of the NT writings is usually taken to mean that they were actually written by apostles, but this is an inadequate conception of this criterion as it functioned in the ancient church. Certainly, some writings were esteemed in the firm conviction that they had been composed by apostles. The Gospel of Matthew and the letters of Paul are good examples, though it would be wrong to think that even in these cases apostolic authorship was the only consideration. Other writings were received as authoritative in the frank recognition that they had only an indirect connection with apostles. Here one may think of Mark and Luke, whose apostolicity was derivative through association with Peter and Paul, respectively. Still other writings found their way into the canon in spite of large uncertainties about their authorship, Hebrews and Revelation being cases in point.[30] And some writings which explicitly claimed apostolic authorship either failed to gain canonical standing altogether (*The Teaching of the Twelve Apostles, Barnabas,* the *Gospel of Peter*) or were acknowledged very tardily and with hesitation (James, 2 Peter, Jude). Obviously, then, apostolic authorship was not the only or even the decisive question in determining the status of a document. It is also clear that apostolicity was not predicated exclusively on apostolic authorship. In fact, the concept "apostolic" was very much broader and could connote, beyond direct apostolic authorship, authorship by followers of apostles, derivation from the general time of the apostles, or even simply an agreement of content with what the church took to be apostolic teaching.[31] Therefore, it is mistaken to confine the idea of apostolicity to literary authenticity. Involving judgments about chronology and content, it refers to what was characteristic of the earliest church.[32] Widespread and important at this criterion was, it must still be said that no NT writing secured canonical standing on the basis of apostolicity alone.

---

30. When Hebrews was accepted in the west, it was viewed mostly as anonymous, but then its canonical standing encouraged the assumption of Pauline authorship. As for Revelation, Dionysius's denial of its apostolic authorship did not cause him to reject it but did subsequently undermine its standing in the east.

31. Ohlig, *Die theologische Begründung*, 57–156.

32. Ibid., 92–93, 152–56 (*Urkirchlichkeit*).

Catholicity

Also considered was the criterion of catholicity: to be recognized as authoritative, a document had to be relevant to the church as a whole and even so intended by its author.[33] Strictly understood, this meant that writings addressed to limited constituencies and not to the church as such were of questionable value. Odd as it may seem, the letters of Paul, though indisputably apostolic, were problematical on the score of catholicity, since Paul had written to specific local communities and not to the church at large. This difficulty was still felt even at the end of the second century.[34] Of course, virtually all the writings which now stand in the canon were, in fact, composed for special groups of recipients and therefore fell short of the ideal of catholicity, but this was not always obvious to the ancient church, and even when it was, other factors could outweigh the want of a general address. What is at work in the use of this criterion is the church's desire to eschew limited, private, and esoteric resources and to prefer broadly accessible and relevant documents.

Orthodoxy

A fundamental, though usually tacit, criterion of canonicity was the agreement of a document's content with the faith of the church—its "orthodoxy."[35] That the authority of a particular writing could be gauged by a standard of orthodoxy means, of course, that the tradition of the church's faith was understood to be somehow extrinsic to the writings which were judged according to it.[36] In this sense, it may be rightly said that ecclesiastical tradition was prior to scripture and served as the touchstone of scripture's authority. But on the other hand, it must also be said that the faith of the Christian community, though capable of independent formulation and access, had itself been shaped from an early time by many of the same documents which ultimately became canonical. By a fruitful synergy, scripture helped to mold the tradition of faith, and the tradition of faith helped to shape the canon of scripture. In practice, therefore, the criterion of orthodoxy resulted

33. Ibid., 225–32.
34. See above, 45 and n. 62.
35. Ohlig, *Die theologische Begründung*, 170–97.
36. Both Irenaeus (*A.H.* 3,4.1–2) and Tertullian (*Praescriptio.* 8–12) urge that the faith may be adequately known and held simply on the basis of the "rule of faith," without recourse to scripture. On the rule of faith, see Hanson, *Tradition in the Early Church*, 75–129; J. N. D. Kelly, *Early Christian Creeds* (New York: Harper & Brothers, 1960), 62–99; J. Mitros, "The Norm of Faith in the Patristic Age," *TS* 29 (1968): 444–71.

in a circular argument: writings were accepted as authoritative if they conformed to the rule of faith, and the rule of faith was validated by appealing, among other things, to the authority of some of the same writings. It is symptomatic of this interplay that the criterion of orthodoxy seems never to have been applied to such literature as the letters of Paul or the Synoptic Gospels. The reason is that these had been valued so long and used so widely that their orthodoxy could only be taken for granted: it would have been nonsensical for the church to have inquired, for example, into the orthodoxy of Paul! If, as the church believed, its tradition of faith derived from the apostles and was therefore really "apostolic tradition," then that tradition could not be sharply differentiated from writings which were also believed to be of apostolic origin. Thus, the criterion of agreement with the faith of the church was used primarily in connection with writings whose authority remained uncertain, and it was applied mainly as a negative standard rather than as a positive argument.[37] Very many early Christian writings were impeccably "orthodox" yet did not gain candidacy as canonical scripture (or, if they did, were not finally canonized).

Traditional Usage

Even more important was the criterion of traditional usage, that is, whether a given document had been customarily employed in the worship and teaching of the various churches.[38] Unlike apostolicity, catholicity, and orthodoxy, which pertain to the internal character of a writing, the principle of traditional usage capitalized on the standing practices of the church. Of course, Christian writings had from an early time been read alongside the Jewish scriptures in the setting of worship. While this practice did not in itself presume or imply that such writings were canonical, it was a tacit recognition of their usefulness, conferred on them a certain authority, and ultimately paved the way for the canonization of some of them.[39] In the nature of the case, the criterion of traditional usage did not come expressly into play until the third and fourth centuries when the church was able to have some retrospect on its own customs. This sort of appeal is especially prominent in Origen, and even more in Eusebius, who consistently

---

37. Ohlig, *Die theologische Begründung*, 195–97.
38. Ibid., 269–95.
39. Ibid., 296–309. On the significance of liturgical reading, cf. J. Ruwet, "Lecture liturgique et livres saints du Nouveau Testament," *Bib* 21 (1940): 378–405.

tried to determine whether a writing had been in public use in the churches from an early time.[40] This criterion was not, however, definitive: many documents which met it quite adequately were not admitted into the canon (e.g., *The Shepherd, 1 Clement, The Teaching of the Twelve Apostles*), while other writings lacking longstanding and broad currency nevertheless did gain canonical recognition, although tardily (e.g., James, 2 Peter, 2 and 3 John). In spite of such exceptions, the canon which eventually emerged does offer a good index of the early Christian writings which in the first several centuries had consistently claimed the attention of the church precisely because those writings had been found useful in nurturing, sustaining, and guiding the faith and life of most Christian communities.

It should be clear that the principles of canonicity adduced in the ancient church were numerous, diverse, and broadly defined, that their application was not systematic or thoroughly consistent, and that they were used in a variety of combinations. So a document without a claim to apostolicity (at least in the stricter senses) could nevertheless be approved as authoritative on the basis of traditional usage. But traditional use was no guarantee of canonical recognition and in a number of cases did not avail for or against. Whereas Paul's letters were apostolic in the strictest authorial sense, they fell far short of the ideal of catholicity. Such variations show that the criteria of canonicity are more representative of the ideals which the church held out for scripture than of the actual character of the writings themselves. In particular the principles of apostolicity, catholicity, and orthodoxy were less the effective reasons for canonical recognition than means of legitimizing the authority that attached to certain documents in virtue of their longstanding use by the church. Therefore, the importance of such principles for the actual history of the canon should not be overestimated.

Inspiration

Before concluding this discussion, some remarks must be made about inspiration, if only because the special authority of the NT writings is so often defended on the ground that they are uniquely inspired.[41] While the ancient church certainly believed that the Jewish Scrip-

40. On Eusebius, see Hanson, *Tradition in the Early Church*, 215–21.
41. See the excellent discussion by P. Achtemeier, *The Inspiration of Scripture: Problems and Proposals* (Philadelphia: Westminster Press, 1980). He notes that, so long as inspiration is taken to be coterminous with the canon, it is necessary to suppose that not only the writings but also the long process of canonization and the final shape of the canon were "inspired."

tures, and above all the prophetic books, were inspired, it did not at first make this claim for Christian writings. But as Christian writings were read alongside the Jewish scriptures and increasingly seen as a counterpart to them, it became ever more customary, beginning about the end of the second century, to assert that Christian writings were also inspired.[42] Nevertheless, in the deliberations of the ancient church about the authority of its writings, we nowhere find an instance of inspiration being used as a criterion of discrimination.[43] Of the literature current in the early church, only a few documents explicitly claimed to be inspired, most notably Revelation, *The Shepherd*, and the *Apocalypse of Peter*. Yet it is apparent in these cases how little consequence this claim had, for neither *The Shepherd* nor the *Apocalypse of Peter* found its way into the canon, and Revelation did so only with difficulty. If inspiration was not a criterion of canonicity in relation to writings which *claimed* to be inspired, so much the less was it a standard for other writings. The reason for this was simply the conviction that the church as a whole was inspired by the Spirit, so that the concept of inspiration was very much broader than the concept of scripture and offered no leverage on the question of the authority of various writings. Inspiration could be and was used to distinguish heretical from orthodox writings: heretical writings were judged not to be inspired because they stood apart from the inspired church. But inspiration could not be used to differentiate orthodox writings into canonical and noncanonical categories.[44] It has been properly noted that "this state of affairs should warn us against any definition of the nature of Holy Scriptures where 'inspiration' so overshadows the process of canonization that the latter is dismissed by a general reference to the providential preservation of twenty-seven inspired books."[45] The NT writings did not become canonical because they were believed to be uniquely inspired; rather, they were judged to be inspired because they had previously commended themselves to the church for other, more particular and practical reasons.

42. Hanson, *Tradition in the Early Church*, 211–13. For Origen's role in the development of a Christian doctrine of the inspiration of Scripture, see Campenhausen, *Formation*, 315–26.
43. K. Stendahl, "Apocalypse of John," 243; cf. 245. This thesis has been fully worked out and confirmed by Kalin, "Argument from Inspiration," summarized in "The Inspired Community: A Glance at Canon History," *CTM* 42 (1971): 542–49. See also A. C. Sundberg, Jr., "The Bible Canon and the Christian Doctrine of Inspiration," *Int* 29 (1975): 352–71.
44. Kalin, "Argument from Inspiration," 230–39.
45. Stendahl, "Apocalypse of John," 244–45.

IV

The Interpretation of
the New Testament as Canon

The interpretation of the NT is normally understood to consist in the interpretation of the individual documents contained in it, studied in and of themselves and with a view to their generative contexts and inherent meanings, but with little or no consideration of their place within the canon. From a historical point of view this is a thoroughly legitimate approach, since the setting of these documents within the canon is secondary and has no direct bearing on the recovery of their original meanings. Nevertheless, this ought not to be confused (as it regularly is) with the interpretation of the NT as such, for the NT is something both more and different than the sum of its parts, and the meaning of the whole may not simply be equated with the cumulative meanings of its constituent elements. The NT is a canon, and though its contents are necessarily and usefully studied independently of this fact, the NT will not be fully understood until it is also understood as a canon. This objective is not achieved only through a reconstruction of the history of the canon, though that is indispensable; the *consequences* of that history must also be evaluated.[1] It is necessary now, therefore, to reflect on the character of the NT as a fixed collection of Christian scriptures.

THE CANON AS
A HERMENEUTICAL CONTEXT

Although for us the NT is an object of interpretation, it is important to realize that the NT is in itself interpretation. The process of interpretation was already at work in the very composition of the writings included in it and may be thought of in a general way as the basic motive of their composition. So, for example, Paul in his letters seeks

1. Among historians of the canon only Harnack (*Origin of the NT*) has tried to trace the consequence of the formation of the canon, but his comments are only marginally relevant here.

to interpret the primitive Christian confession for Gentile Christian groups, and the author of Mark gives a distinctive theological interpretation of the traditions about Jesus. Such early writings as these became, in turn, the subject of interpretation in other writings. Thus, Matthew and Luke may appropriately be viewed as interpretive revisions of their sources, including Mark, and the pseudonymous Pauline letters are in their various ways interpretations of Paul's teaching. These examples show that the NT does not consist from first to last of what might be called "primary traditions" or "primary texts"; rather, the NT incorporates various stages of tradition and interpretation, text, and commentary. Each document was in its original setting an effort to apprehend and adapt tradition in a new situation.

The process of interpretation was at work, however, not only in the composition of these writings but equally in their subsequent histories. They themselves came into broad use and gained authority so far as they were susceptible to appropriation in later situations and so proved their persistent value to the church. Indeed, their capacity for continuing reinterpretation was the necessary condition for the religious authority which accrued to them, in virtue of which they came to be seen as scripture and then were made part of the canon. This authority did not simply reside in the documents but depended on what they were understood to mean by the communities which read them. So, for example, Paul's letters could be received as authoritative only on the presumption that they had relevance and meaning beyond the particular circumstances of the churches addressed by Paul. The Gospel of John did not acquire any broad authority until the church found a perspective by which to comprehend it along with the more traditional Gospels (i.e., by viewing it as "the spiritual Gospel"). And the authority of Revelation was much disputed so long as its meaning was in debate; at least in the eastern church, its authority could be granted only if it were allegorically interpreted. Religious authority was therefore a function of the interaction between the texts and their readers—that is, of interpretation. For this reason the history of the canon cannot finally be differentiated from the history of interpretation. The canon consists of those writings which came into traditional use and authoritative esteem precisely because they lent themselves to meaningful appropriation by Christian communities in later and different circumstances.

But if the NT writings are interpretations of prior traditions, and if they were valued and preserved through an ongoing process of interpretation, then it must also be emphasized that their consolidation into a canon was an event with far-reaching hermeneutical consequences of its own. In the nature of the case, canonization entails a recontextualization of the documents incorporated into the canon. They are abstracted from both their generative and traditional settings and redeployed as parts of a new literary whole; henceforth, they are known and read in terms of this collection. In this way their historically secondary context becomes their hermeneutically primary context. The consequences of this shift for the interpretation of the NT writings were various but momentous. For one thing, the formation of the canon served to obscure its own history and to relativize the historical and particular character of the texts which belong to it. Once the collection had come into being, it could be taken as a thing in itself and considered independently of the forces which led to its creation and independently of other documents which, though having close historical or literary relationships with the canonical documents, were not included in the canon. Furthermore, the creation of the canon had a leveling effect upon its contents: within the canon each document appears to have the same status and value as any other. Although canonization marks out a clear boundary between the writings in the canon and those outside it, it signals no distinctions among its own contents and indeed militates against them. Consequently, for example, within the canon 2 Peter and Romans appear to have the same standing, even though in the precanonical period 2 Peter did not remotely approximate Romans in the extent of its use or value in the church. More important still, the canon creates a presumption of unity and coherence among its contents and inevitably encourages a synoptic reading of them. Thus, the canon operates to refocus the meaning of individual documents, as each is read with a view to the others and in the light of the collection as a whole. This has two broad results. On the one hand, it works to minimize the meaning(s) peculiar to particular texts within the collection and so to mask differences or incongruities among them. On the other hand, it generates a new range of meanings on the basis of the intertextual relationships established by the canon. Since the canon has such results, it cannot be regarded only as an anthology; in its actual effects the canon is a hermeneutical medium which by its very nature influences the understanding of its contents. The hermeneutical force of the NT canon is not, however, merely tacit or fortuitous. It is also intimated by formal features which characterize the discrete collections within the canon and by the structure and contours of the canon as a whole. Some of these aspects of the canon deserve special notice.

The collection of four Gospels, as noted earlier, represents a compromise which the ancient church devised to mediate between the ideal of a single, self-consistent, theologically adequate gospel and the actual availability of many gospel-type documents. The collection aims at an inclusive yet not exhaustive witness to the Christ event. In this respect the collection continues along the path of the NT Gospel writers themselves, each of whom brought together diverse traditions about Jesus in order to provide fuller and more pointed portrayals of him. But in another way the grouping of four Gospels violates the intentions of the Gospel writers, each of whom apparently meant to offer an independent and self-sufficient account. In effect, the collection introduces a principle of mutual correction and limitation whereby each Gospel is deprived of pre-eminence or complete validity. This is borne out by the peculiar way in which the church referred to these writings: all four were subsumed under a single heading, "the gospel," and each was designated as the Gospel "according to" (*kata*) its ostensible author. That is, none of them was understood to be or to contain "the gospel" pure and simple. If in this fashion both the commonality and individuality of these writings are affirmed, their value is nevertheless relativized in relation to each other and in relation to "the gospel" itself.[2] Hence, the *gospel message* ("the gospel") is not reducible to any one Gospel *document* but stands beyond them as the subject of their corporate witness.[3] As a collection, then, the Gospels stand in a creative tension with each other: instead of four Gospels, there is a fourfold Gospel. It seems clear, furthermore, that at or near the inception of this collection its form was taken to be an essential correlate of its proper understanding (cf. Irenaeus), such that theological meaning and authority were vested in the collection rather than in the single documents taken by themselves. Thus, the collection, by its very form, provides a critical principle for its interpretation.

Something similar can be said about the other major collection which belongs to the NT—the letters of Paul—though for different reasons. The assumption which prompted the circulation and collection of Paul's letters—namely, that in spite of their particularity they have relevance and value for the church at large—was given expression in an early,

2. Thus, the ancient church was relatively indifferent to the precise order of the Gospels, and various orders are attested in the early period.
3. See R. Morgan, "The Hermeneutical Significance of Four Gospels," *Int* 35 (1981): 376–88.

perhaps original, edition of the letters which presented them as letters to seven churches, the number seven indicating their universal pertinence.[4] This connotation was not lost even when the letters were counted individually and the collection was expanded to include fourteen letters (two times seven). Thus, the hermeneutical intention of the collection is embodied in its outward form. But more than this, the Pauline corpus, even in its earliest known editions, incorporates pseudonymous letters which interpret Pauline teaching. Recognizing this, the historical-critical effort to lay hold of Paul's teaching attends to the authentic letters alone, and properly so, since the historical Paul is certainly not identical with the canonical Paul. But this distinction was not drawn by the ancient church, which esteemed Paul precisely in terms of the sorts of universalizing and ecclesiological perspectives that gain their clearest expression in the pseudonymous letters, and not in terms of the radical and controversial aspects of Paul's teaching that belong to the authentic letters. Thus, in content as well as in form, the collection of Paul's letters offers guidance for the theological interpretation of the apostle's teaching. From the point of view of the corpus and of the canon in which it was included, the meaning and authority of Paul for the church are not contingent on individual letters, nor even on the authentic ones alone, but inhere in the collection as a whole.

Unlike the letters of Paul the catholic letters had very diverse individual histories and were brought together as a discrete group only in the fourth century. Therefore, in spite of the close literary, historical, or theological relationships which exist among some of them, the grouping of these seven letters is artificial. But it is not arbitrary. The significance of this collection can be inferred from an early arrangement which, with one change, subsequently became standard: James, 1 and 2 Peter, 1, 2, and 3 John, Jude. The rationale for this order appears to lie in a correlation made by the ancient church between these letters and Paul's reference (Gal. 2:9) to the "pillar apostles," whom he names in the order James, Peter, John. Since Gal. 2:1–10 and Acts 15:1–35 were read as proof of the agreement of the apostles and of the unanimity of apostolic preaching, the gathering up of these "catholic letters" and their use alongside Paul's letters gave documentary expression to the idea of a corporate and unitary teaching deriving from principal apostolic mentors.[5] The formal legitimation of the col-

4. See above, 42.
5. See esp. D. Lührmann, "Gal. 2.9 und die katholischen Briefe," ZNW 72 (1981): 65–87.

lection is derived from Paul, but at the same time this collection serves to counterbalance the imposing legacy of Pauline literature, both implicitly and explicitly (cf. James, 2 Peter). Here, too, then, the significance of the collection goes beyond the meanings of the individual documents within it and is a function of its form as much as of its contents.

The larger structure of the NT canon was not given along with the documents that were canonized. It had to be created. But since the canon is for the most part a "collection of collections," the larger structure of the canon was mainly a matter of arranging pre-existing groups of writings, and the options were therefore limited. Even so, the shape which the canon assumed deserves comment. Ancient lists and editions of the canonical writings almost invariably placed the Gospels first. This priority owes nothing to literary chronology but is due, rather, to the pre-eminent importance of their subject, Jesus, who was the focus of the church's faith, its point of origin and persistent reference. Moreover, the tradition of his words and deeds had served from the beginning as the primary authority of the church's faith. Therefore, the primacy of the Gospels within the canon had ample justification. But it was much less obvious how the other collections might be arranged, and some variations were typical as the canon took full form. In some early lists and editions of the NT the catholic letters preceded the letters of Paul, but followed in others. Acts, lacking a place in any of the larger collections, was most closely associated at first with the catholic letters, either preceding or following them. The key to this association, and also the reason why Acts came into popularity at all and eventually gained canonical standing, lies in the use made of Acts beginning in the late second century. It was a helpful document for demonstrating over-against heterodox movements the unity of the primitive church and the consensus of its apostolic leaders, and thus in substantiating the claim of an original, normative body of apostolic teaching. Consequently, it was most naturally brought into relation with writings purportedly deriving from those original apostolic figures. But soon enough the same logic led to the placement of Acts as a frontispiece to the entire range of apostolic letters, including Paul's, for there it gave a perspective from which all of them might be read as expressions of a unitary teaching of the primitive apostles and Paul. In its standard position within the canon, however, Acts plays another and equally important role: it provides the bridgework between Gospels and apostolic letters. By its content it is very well

78

suited to this purpose because it explicitly correlates the teaching and authority of the apostles with Jesus himself and emphasizes their foundational importance for the church. These features allow Acts both to warrant the standing of apostolic letters within the canon and to articulate a rationale for a bipartite canon consisting of Gospel *and* Apostle.[6] In this way the principle of apostolicity, which had been invoked on behalf of these writings during the earlier period, was finally built into the structure of the canon itself, so that the substance of the canon gains legitimacy from its form.

This survey of the more prominent formal features of the canon and its component collections should suffice to show that the canon is a hermeneutical construct not only by circumstance but to some extent also by design. This design urges the coherence of the several collections within themselves and with each other and so promotes the interpretation of each text with a view to other texts. In this way, the import of single documents is qualified and revised by the larger whole, while at the same time the larger whole gives rise to new meanings through the textual configurations created by the canon. *Thus, the canon itself is a locus of meaning.* The meaning which accrues to a document within the canonical matrix, its "canonical sense," is not necessarily identical or even continuous with its intrinsic, historical meaning but sometimes exceeds or even contravenes the significance a document can be said to have in its own right. For example, since the Gospel of Luke and the Book of Acts were composed together as a continuous narrative in two volumes, it does not seem that the author meant to write a Gospel in the same sense that the other Gospel writers did, or that what we call the Gospel of Luke is rightly part of the fourfold Gospel. The separation of Luke and Acts in the canon violates the author's intention and confers on each part of his work meanings and functions they did not originally bear. Likewise, the canonical presentation of Paul's authentic letters in the company of pseudonymous Pauline letters, with the whole framed by the legends about Paul in Acts and by the catholic epistles, inevitably qualifies Paul's most incisive ideas and obscures the particularity of his concerns. Nevertheless, the "canonical sense" which arises through these juxtapositions is a dimension of meaning which belongs to the NT and is specifically characteristic of the NT as such, that is, as canon.

If the canon does function, either by circumstance or design, as a

6. On the significance of Acts in this regard, see R. W. Funk, "The New Testament as Tradition and Canon," in *Parables and Presence* (Philadelphia: Fortress Press, 1982), 179.

hermeneutical framework, it is a different and more difficult question whether and to what extent the interpretation of the NT should be predicated on its character as canon and should attend to specifically canonical meanings. Historical criticism has traditionally disregarded the canon as irrelevant for the interpretation of individual documents, and this disregard is for the most part legitimate within the objectives of historical interpretation.[7] But in recent years there has been a growing interest in the relevance of the canon for the use of Scripture in the church—that is, for theological exegesis and the articulation of a biblical theology. This interest, which has gained the label "canonical criticism," has been pursued so far almost exclusively in connection with the OT but in markedly different ways by its chief exponents, B. S. Childs and J. A. Sanders. Childs has argued that the theological interpretation of scripture ought to proceed on the basis of the "final (canonical) form" of a given text and with persistent attention to its "full canonical context"—that is, the way that text is related to all other texts in the canon. Thus, the *literary* context of the canon is made the basis and touchstone of interpretation, rather than the original historical context of the canonical documents.[8] Sanders, however, has focused not on the final form and fixed canonical context of the documents but upon the *process* of canonization—that is, the hermeneutical dynamics by which authoritative traditions were not only stabilized but were, time and again, revised and adapted, reformulated and rewritten, in order to make them freshly relevant to the ever-changing circumstances of the religious community. Here canonical criticism is a matter of discerning the hermeneutical processes lying behind and within the canon and using them as paradigms for its modern appropriation.[9] Different as these programs are, both urge a renewed appreciation of the canon for the task of theological interpretation.

The question of the hermeneutical significance of the canon has scarcely been raised for the NT in terms of the perspectives employed

7. But note the sensible warnings of L. E. Keck, "Is the New Testament a Field of Study? From Outler to Overbeck and Back," *Second Century* 1 (1981): 19–35. He rightly comments on the importance of the canon even for historical criticism.

8. Childs's position is sketched in his *Biblical Theology in Crisis* (Philadelphia: Westminster Press, 1970) and is fully represented in his *Introduction to the Old Testament as Scripture* (Philadelphia: Fortress Press, 1979). A series of critical appraisals, together with responses by Childs, may be found in *JSOT* 16 (1980) and in *HBT* 2 (1980).

9. See J. A. Sanders, *Torah and Canon* (Philadelphia: Fortress Press, 1972); idem, "Adaptable for Life: The Nature and Function of the Canon," in *Magnalia Dei, The Mighty Acts of God: Essays on the Bible and Archaeology in Memory of G. E. Wright*, ed. F. M. Cross, W. E. Lemke, and P. Miller (Garden City, N.Y.: Doubleday & Co., 1976), 531–60.

in the canonical criticism of the OT.[10] Yet those perspectives cannot have quite the same force for the NT, chiefly because the history of the NT literature is much less protracted and complex. For the NT documents there is less distance and less difference between early traditions and their final textual redactions, and between final textual redactions and the formation of the canon. Hence, an emphasis on the "final form" of a text (Childs) or on the long and varied history of the adaptation of tradition (Sanders) has considerably less relevance for the NT canon than for the OT canon. Nevertheless, canonical criticism has rightly called attention to the fact that the canon as such constitutes a vehicle of meaning and that the meaning which belongs to the canonical context needs to be appreciated in itself if the nature of the canon is to be fully understood.

While it is important to recognize the hermeneutical aspects of the canon and the meanings which accrue to the texts as a result of their configuration within the canon, it is by no means clear, as some advocates of canonical criticism maintain, that only the "canonical sense" of the texts is relevant for theological exegesis or that the canon as a whole provides the proper context for interpretation. The canonical sense of the texts is only one among other senses which have a different basis but belong equally to the canon.[11] Each document in the canon draws upon and to some extent reproduces traditions, whether oral or written, which were in themselves authoritative for the Christian communities that cultivated them, and the meaning of these traditions had nothing to do with a larger literary context, still less with a canon of scripture. So far as such traditions have been absorbed into documents which later became canonical, those traditions comprise a level of meaning in the canon but one very different from the canonical meaning. Beyond this, there is also an authorial level of meaning in the NT, and this consists of the meaning we can ascribe to the intentions of the writer of each document. This must be distinguished both from the meaning of such traditions as the author employed and from the significance of the author's work in its subsequent canonical setting. Yet another level of meaning is provided by the church's understand-

---

10. Recent studies along these lines include R. E. Brown, *The Critical Meaning of the Bible* (New York: Paulist Press, 1981), esp. 23–44; J. D. G. Dunn, "Levels of Canonical Authority," *HBT* (1981): 13–60; R. W. Funk, "The New Testament as Tradition and Canon," 151–86; A. C. Outler, "The Logic of Canon-Making and the Tasks of Canon Criticism," in *Texts and Testaments*, ed. W. E. March, 263–76. See also the appended note, p. 92 below.
11. See esp. Dunn, "Levels of Canonical Authority," 18–27.

ing of its scripture, and this ecclesiastical level of meaning is not necessarily to be identified with the traditional, authorial, or canonical meanings which may be assigned to the canonical writings. Indeed, it is not *in* the canon in quite the same way, for it lies in the interaction between the canon of scripture and the ongoing life of the Christian community.[12] Among these various levels of meaning, it is not obvious that the canonical sense has, or ought to be granted, any special preeminence, let alone exclusive validity. So far as it is distinctive, the canonical sense does not spring from the intention of any biblical writer. Rather, it arises through the collocation of diverse texts, and what it reflects above all are the hermeneutical perspectives of the church which brought these texts together, drew a boundary around them, and provided structural relationships among them. The canonical sense is not for this reason to be either minimized or absolutized. To the extent that the form of the canon preserves and promotes a way of reading its contents which accentuates the meanings they had come to have for the church, it surely has relevance for the tasks of theological exegesis. Yet it was not the form of the canon, or the canonical sense, that first elevated these particular documents to the status of scripture but the meanings that were attached to them individually or in small groupings during the earlier history of their interpretation and use, and these meanings bore a much closer relationship to the authorial sense. In any case, the canonical sense of any writing is not something that can be isolated from its authorial meanings: even if it is distinct, it is not independent, for it results from the interplay between the text and its context. Therefore, an adequate hermeneutic of the canon cannot be precritically indifferent to detailed historical criticism. But also, historical criticism cannot fully explicate the meaning of the NT without attending to the hermeneutical import of the canon.

THE CANON
AS A THEOLOGICAL PROBLEM

The theological problem of the canon, though not unrelated to the hermeneutical issues already discussed, is focused more specifically on the question: How does the NT canon possess and exercise normative authority for Christianity? This question has been inescapably posed both by investigations of the history of the canon and by the historical exegesis of the canonical texts. It has become the subject of

12. See esp. Brown, *Critical Meaning*, 34–43.

heated controversy in recent decades because it touches directly on far-reaching differences in the conception and use of the canon among different confessional bodies within Christianity, above all, Roman Catholicism and Protestantism.[13] The problem can be conveniently explored under the following three leading aspects.

The Scope of the Canon

In the light of modern knowledge about the history of the canon and the character of its contents, it is difficult to justify the limitation of the canon to precisely the twenty-seven documents which have traditionally belonged to it. The reasons for this are several. First, as the canon took shape, only such documents as had survived and were still available could be considered for inclusion in it. But some of Paul's letters, the written sources behind the Gospels, and no doubt many other pieces of early Christian literature were simply lost. In this sense, the potential content of the canon was affected from the outset by the accidents of literary preservation. Second, the crucible for the long process of canon formation was provided by a complex interplay of historical circumstances, theological controversies, traditions of interpretation, regional usages, judgments of ecclesiastical authorities, and even the technical aspects of book manufacture and textual transmission. The scope of the canon is therefore indebted to a wide range of contingent historical factors and from a historical standpoint is largely fortuitous. Third, the limits of the canon cannot any longer be defended on the basis of the explicit warrants adduced on its behalf by the ancient church. Historical criticism has shown that the ancient church was most often mistaken in its claims that the canonical writings were written by apostles, while the history of the canon makes it doubtful that theoretical criteria (apostolicity, catholicity, etc.) were effective reasons for canonization.[14] For all these reasons, the traditional boundaries of the NT canon have been deprived of clear and self-evident validity.[15]

13. Some of the most important studies have been collected and evaluated by E. Käsemann, *Das Neue Testament als Kanon. Dokumentation und kritische Analyze zur gegenwärtigen Diskussion* (Göttingen: Vandenhoeck & Ruprecht, 1970). Useful broad assessments of the main issues are given by N. Appel, *Kanon und Kirche. Die Kanonkrise im heutigen protestantismus als kontroverstheologisches Problem* (Paderborn: Bonifacius-Druckerei, 1964), representing a Catholic viewpoint; I. Lönning, *Kanon im Kanon*, representing a Protestant perspective.

14. See above, 67–72.

15. Thus, e.g., H. Braun, "Hebt die heutige neutestamentlich-exegetische Forschung den Kanon auf?" in *Gesammelte Studien zum Neuen Testament und seiner Umwelt* (Tübingen: Mohr, Siebeck, 1962), 310–34; W. G. Kümmel, "Notwendigkeit und Grenze"; A. Sand, "Die Diskrepanz zwischen historischer Zufälligkeit und normativem Charakter des neutestamentlichen Kanons als hermeneutisches Problem," *MThZ* 24 (1973): 147–60.

In this situation, two different claims have been advanced in support of the limits of the canon: Protestant scholars have typically asserted that the canonical literature has an intrinsic and self-authenticating authority which impresses itself on the conscientious reader, whereas Catholic scholars have typically maintained that the canon derives its authority from official recognition by the church. These alternatives take a more historical form in the claims either that the canon evolved more or less spontaneously through the religious experience and intuition of the early Christian communities, or that it was carefully and deliberately constructed by the church. But neither view is fully adequate to the actual history of the canon. For example, the judgments of bishops and councils in the fourth and fifth centuries did not merely ratify a status which these writings had already secured for themselves,[16] since some of the writings then recognized as canonical had not been widely used or everywhere received as authoritative. So, as a closed collection and in respect of its specific limits, the canon is very much a product of the church. Yet the high regard which attached from an early time and almost everywhere to the Synoptic Gospels and the letters of Paul owed nothing to official decisions, and the later church could only acknowledge their authority, not decide it. To this extent the canon, though not yet as a definitive collection, was functionally prior to the church, which is grounded in the primitive witness to the Christ event.[17] Hence, the relationship between the authority of the canon and the authority of the church is historically ambiguous.

The burden of much recent Protestant thinking has been to admit that the canon is "factually" or "historically" closed while insisting that the limits of the canon prescribed in the ancient church are not binding and that the scope of the canon remains in principle open to revision.[18] This view does not actually intend any alteration of the traditional boundaries of the canon. It aims instead to assert and preserve the critical independence of scripture over-against the church: when the canon is taken to be a "strictly dogmatic reality, that is, when not only the boundaries of the canon but also the meaning of its canonicity are

16. Thus, among others, K. Aland, *Problem of the NT Canon*, 18–24; H. Diem, *Das Problem des Schriftkanons* (Zollikon-Zürich: Evangelischer Verlag, 1952), 6–7; F. Hahn, "Die Heilige Schrift als älteste christliche Tradition und als Kanon," *EvTh* 40 (1980): 462–63.

17. Kümmel, "Notwendigkeit und Grenze," 24–34.

18. Ibid., 249–59; Diem, *Das Problem des Schriftkanons*, 15–16; W. Marxsen, *The New Testament as the Church's Book* (Philadelphia: Fortress Press, 1972); G. Ebeling, *The Problem of Historicity in the Church and Its Proclamation* (Philadelphia: Fortress Press, 1967), 62–64; idem, "'Sola Scriptura' and Tradition," in *Word of God and Tradition* (Philadelphia: Fortress Press, 1968), 113–21; Lönning, *Kanon im Kanon*, 263–68.

considered as beyond all discussion, Protestantism has already become Catholic in principle, for it is then founded upon the infallibility of a doctrinal decision of early Catholicism" (that is, about the limits of the canon).[19] Since apart from an infallible teaching office of the church there can be no certainty about the correctness of the traditional contents of the canon, the limits of the canon are necessarily provisional according to Protestant principles. Still, it can be maintained among Protestant scholars that the canon must at least theoretically have limits because reliable testimony to a historical locus of revelation entails chronological and spatial proximity.[20] This very delicately fashioned position finds little appreciation among Catholic scholars who, while acknowledging the appearance of contingency in the history of the canon and the fragility of the criteria of canonicity, fully affirm the traditional limits of the canon as the authoritative work of the church, acting in accordance with historic usage, true teaching, and providential guidance.[21] Here the canon of scripture and the teaching authority of the church form an indivisible unity. It is worth noting, however, that prior to the Council of Trent (1564) and its dogmatic definition of the canon it was not uncommon for the proper limits of the canon to be debated, especially in regard to those writings that had also been disputed in the ancient church.

The Nature of the Canon as Norm

The concept of the canon and its normative function have been called into question even more by the exegesis of NT texts than by the history of the canon. It has been the extraordinary result of modern historical study to show that among the canonical texts there is a wide range of theological orientations which are not only diverse but to some extent also incompatible and mutually contradictory. Within the scope of the traditional canon, Jewish Christianity, various forms of Hellenistic Christianity, apocalyptic Christianity, and early catholic Christianity each finds its literary representations and articulates its particular claims.[22] In this respect the NT canon may indeed reflect

19. Ebeling, *Problem of Historicity*, 63.

20. Kümmel, "Notwendigkeit und Grenze," 247–49.

21. So, e.g., P. Lengsfeld, *Überlieferung. Tradition und Schrift in der evangelischen und katholischen Theologie der Gegenwart* (Paderborn: Bonifacius-Druckerei, 1960), 112–18; Appel, *Kanon und Kirche*, 115–20; R. E. Brown, "Canonicity," *JBC* (1968): 533.

22. The most provocative and influential sketch of this state of affairs has been furnished by E. Käsemann, "The Canon of the New Testament and the Unity of the Church," in idem, *Essays on New Testament Themes* (London: SCM Press, 1964; Philadelphia: Fortress Press), 95–107. For a detailed exposition of the varieties of theological positions in the NT, see J. D. G. Dunn, *Unity and Diversity in the New Testament* (Philadelphia: Westminster Press, 1977).

the theological variegations and internal controversies of early Christianity, but so far as it also represents divergent theological standpoints as having canonical force, the canon as such cannot serve as a decisive theological norm. Instead of providing a firm basis for the unity of Christianity, the canon merely legitimizes the multiplicity of discordant confessions, each of which may appeal to the NT with equal right.[23] By throwing into sharp relief the extent of theological diversity within the canon, historical-critical exegesis has made it impossible to sustain the formal and legal understanding of the canon, widespread in Protestantism and Catholicism alike, according to which the canon is a doctrinal unity possessing equal authority in all its parts, with theological inconsistencies being ruled out in principle.[24] In practical terms, this means that a theological claim cannot now be vindicated by the simple shibboleth, "The NT says . . . ," not because the NT does not say it, but because it says much else besides and not with straightforward consistency. Taken as a whole, therefore, the canon cannot constitute a sharply effective theological norm.

But once a formal, dogmatic conception of the canon is given up in frank recognition of its inner diversities, it becomes necessary to conceive its normative function in another way. This is often done by Protestant scholars by appealing to a material principle (*Sachkriterium*) or center (*Sachmitte*) which is represented as the essential and controlling element in the NT. Such a principle or center is commonly called a "canon in the canon." The specification of a "canon in the canon" does not involve any literary reduction of the formal canon to a smaller and more consistent collection of writings but aims to provide a hermeneutical criterion by which to discern the fundamental meaning of scripture and to allow that meaning to operate as a theological standard. Thus, a "canon in the canon" signifies an actual canon (in the sense of theological *norm*) within the formal canon (in the sense of *list* or *collection* of writings).[25]

The usefulness and indeed indispensability of such a norm is widely admitted in Protestant circles, but efforts to formulate it have been various in method and result. Some, relying on historical criteria, have suggested that the original preaching of Jesus, or the oldest recover-

23. Käsemann, "The Canon"; cf. also Käsemann, "Is the Gospel Objective?" in *Essays on NT Themes*, 48–62, esp. 54–58, and *Das Neue Testament als Kanon*, 402. Of course, the diversity of the canon is not the sole cause of confessional diversities, as rightly noted by G. Ebeling, "The New Testament and the Multiplicity of Confessions," in *Word of God and Tradition*, 148–59.

24. Käsemann, "The Canon of the New Testament"; Ebeling, " 'Sola Scriptura' and Tradition," 142–44.

25. On the concept and its history, cf. Lönning, *Kanon im Kanon*, passim, but esp. 16–30.

able form of the kerygma, is the authoritative element in the canon. Others, disavowing historical criteria, have located the essential meaning of the NT in a theological principle, such as the justification of the ungodly or the radical questioning of human existence or, in the well-known formula of Luther, "what preaches and promotes Christ."[26]

Catholic scholars have been roundly critical of the interest in a canon in the canon and see it as a clear admission of the inadequacy of the Protestant principle of *sola scriptura,* "scripture alone." They object specifically to the reductionism, selectivity, and arbitrary subjectivity it seems to entail and insist on the need to affirm the unity and coherence of the canon as a whole.[27] These objections are intelligible and not altogether misplaced, but the proposed alternative is untenable and represents the very problem which creates the need for a canon in the canon. How is it possible, once the theological diversity of the canon is admitted, to give equal authority to all the canonical documents? Either historical results will not be taken seriously, or a perspective will be found outside the canon which determines how scripture is to be interpreted, in which case the authority of the canon will be given up anyway. The essential difference between the typically Protestant and Catholic viewpoints is that Protestant scholars are intent on finding an interpretive principle within the canon while Catholic scholars look for it outside the canon, in the authoritative teaching of the church. Each view is in its own way an admission that the formal canon does not and cannot serve as an effective theological norm.

Of course, on the question of a canon in the canon, it is an oversimplification to speak of a strict division between Protestant and Catholic scholarship. There are Catholic scholars who see the need for some form of intracanonical discrimination and Protestant scholars who are suspicious of the idea. But it needs to be emphasized that the concept of a canon in the canon is badly misconstrued if it is taken to be a

26. For a survey of the proposals, see W. Schrage, "Der Frage nach der Mitte und dem Kanon im Kanon des Neuen Testaments in der neueren Diskussion," in *Rechtfertigung: Festschrift E. Käsemann,* ed. J. Friedrich, W. Pohlmann, and P. Stuhlmacher (Tübingen: Mohr/Siebeck, 1976), 415–42. On Luther in particular, see D. W. Lotz, "*Sola Scriptura:* Luther on Biblical Authority," *Int* 35 (1981): 258–73.

27. Thus, e.g., Lengsfeld, *Überlieferung,* 146–47; Appel, *Kanon und Kirche,* 253–65; F. Mussner, "Die Mitte des Evangeliums in neutestamentlicher Sicht," in *Gott und Welt: Festgabe K. Rahner,* ed. J. B. Metz et al. (Freiburg, 1964), 492–514; H. Küng, "'Early Catholicism' in the New Testament as a Problem in Controversial Theology," in idem, *The Council in Action: Theological Reflections on the Second Vatican Council* (New York and London: Sheed & Ward, 1963), 159–95. For an overview and criticism of Catholic objections, see W. G. Kümmel, "Das Problem der 'Mitte' des Neuen Testaments," in *L'évangile hier et aujourd'hui. Mélanges offerts F. J. Leenhardt* (Geneva: Labor et Fides, 1968), 71–85; and Käsemann, *Das Neue Testament als Kanon,* 371–82.

question of the whole canon versus parts of the canon rather than a question about the interpretation of the whole—that is, a hermeneutical question.[28] Nevertheless, the terminology runs the risk of creating confusion between "scripture" on the one hand and "hermeneutics" on the other.

What is fundamentally at stake in the debate about a canon in the canon is whether there can be any opposition between the canon and the church, that is, whether and how scripture can exercise a critical and corrective function over-against the church and so really be a norm in itself. In this sense the idea of a canon in the canon actually represents the intention of the *sola scriptura* principle, even though it disavows a formal notion of the canon. Thus, it can be seen that the two concerns, about the internal center of the canon and about the external limits of the canon, are intimately related: both aim to distinguish the authority of scripture from the authority of the church and to maintain the autonomy of scripture. For when the outer boundaries of the canon are regarded as absolutely fixed, the theologically normative force of the canon is reduced, and correspondingly, when the critical function of the canon is emphasized, its precise limits are relativized.[29] Since the formal canon is unquestionably characterized by theological variety, nothing less than a canon in the canon—a selective principle of interpretation—can provide the sharp definition required of a theological norm.

The dilemma between the generous diversity of the formal canon and the stinting specificity of a canon in the canon is sometimes resolved in a different way, by taking the canonical standing of different theological viewpoints as a positive endorsement of a broad confessional pluralism within Christianity.[30] On this view the multiplicity of confessions claiming the name Christian is less a fact to be regretted than it is a fact which has typified Christianity from the beginning and belongs to its very nature. This views falls outside the terms of the debate in continental scholarship and belongs to the religiously pluralistic Anglo-American setting. Still, it is a useful reminder that the attempt to find in the canon a thoroughly uniform and coherent norm may be contrary to the aims even of the ancient church, which canonized a range of theological positions, sometimes in a deliberately ecumenical spirit (e. g., Hebrews, Revelation, the Gospel of John), and

28. Käsemann, *Das Neue Testament als Kanon*, 376.
29. Lönning, *Kanon im Kanon*, 268–71.
30. F. V. Filson, *Which Books Belong to the Bible?*, 133–34; Dunn, *Unity and Diversity*, 374–82.

consistently demurred from reductionistic proposals aimed at strict consistency (Marcion's *Apostolikon*, Tatian's *Diatessaron*). From this viewpoint, then, the canon's normative function is not to preclude diversity but only to limit its scope within broad but definite perimeters.

Apart from the controversy within NT scholarship about the theological legitimacy and precise character of a canon in the canon, it is widely recognized that in fact every interpreter of the NT and every confessional standpoint within Christianity operates, consciously or unconsciously, with a hermeneutical perspective or principle which serves to organize the canonical writings in a certain way and to elicit from them a particular pattern of meaning.[31] This is not only inevitable but necessary if the canon is to play a role in theological reflection and not remain unmanageably and meaninglessly diffuse. Whether these principles or perspectives should be called canons in the canon is unimportant. Their effect is the same: to develop from the formal de jure canon a working de facto canon. Yet just here the importance of the formal canon in all its diversity appears, for although it requires a reduction and specification of its meaning in order to exercise a normative function, it nevertheless resists the absolutizing of any particular appropriation and so maintains the potentialities of interpretation against dogmatic foreclosures. Thus, in its own way the formal canon works to insure the autonomy and authority of scripture and of the gospel it mediates.

Scripture and Tradition

A third dimension of the theological problem of the canon in modern study lies in the relationship between scripture and tradition. The fixed distinction between scripture and tradition, and the standing opposition of the Protestant principle of *sola scriptura* to the Catholic watchword of *scriptura et traditio,* have lost their basis and application. Both the history of the canon and exegetical work have had a part in this.

The history of the canon indicates clearly enough that the contents of the NT were determined by the church on the basis of tradition. Perhaps the most powerful force was the tradition of ecclesiastical usage, but the writings which came to canonical standing on this account were buttressed by traditional ideas of authorship and validated

31. See, e.g., Aland, *Problem of the NT Canon,* 28–31; Dunn, *Unity and Diversity,* 374–75; J. Barr, *Holy Scripture* (Philadelphia: Westminster Press, 1983), 70–73.

89

through traditional conceptions and formulations of the faith. Therefore, to acknowledge the authority of the canon is to acknowledge the
authority of the tradition which gave birth to it: one cannot have scripture without also having tradition. This point has been regularly made
by Catholic scholars against the Protestant habit of opposing scripture
to tradition, and it is a point increasingly admitted by Protestant scholars.[32] This admission is often accompanied by legitimate reservations,
such as that it is an oversimplification to view canonization merely as
a matter of ecclesiastical decisions, or that by creating a canon of
scripture the church was deliberately submitting itself to scripture as
a norm. Still, the basic fact remains that the canon of scripture is
predicated on the tradition of the ancient church.

But exegesis also has undermined the distinction between scripture
and tradition by showing that the individual documents of the canon
are themselves, to a greater or lesser extent, products of tradition.
This is pre-eminently true of the Gospels, as form criticism has dem-
onstrated, but in the epistles too there is a deep indebtedness to
kerygmatic, liturgical, paraenetic, and exegetical traditions. Indeed,
the farther back one penetrates into early Christianity, the more per-
vasive tradition is. Furthermore, the NT not only embodies earlier
tradition but actually exhibits the development of tradition among its
own contents, as for example in the appropriation of Mark by Matthew
and Luke, or in the treatment of Pauline teaching among the pseudo-
Pauline letters. Historically speaking, then, tradition precedes scripture, is presumed by scripture, and persists in scripture. As a result,
the problem of "scripture and tradition," which has customarily belonged to historical and systematic theology, has entered the field of
exegesis, and exegesis has made it impossible to sustain the dichotomy
between the two. Therefore, it is increasingly common for Protestant
scholars to characterize the canonical literature as "a specific form of
tradition" or as a "freezing" or "transcription" of tradition at a particular stage.[33] This way of speaking marks an approximation toward the
Catholic distinction between scripture and tradition in terms of written
and unwritten tradition.

The recognition of the historical importance of tradition in contrib-

32. See, e.g., Cullman, "The Tradition," in *The Early Church*, 59–99, esp. 87–98; Ebeling, *Problem of Historicity*, 62–63, and " 'Sola Scriptura' and Tradition," 113–14; Marxsen, *New Testament as the Church's Book*, 16–20.

33. Ebeling, " 'Sola Scriptura' and Tradition," 108; C. F. Evans, *Is Holy Scripture Christian?* (London: SCM Press, 1971), 18–19; E. Best, "Scripture, Tradition, and the Canon of the New Testament," *BJRL* 61 (1979): 258–89, esp. 264–67; Hahn, "Die Heilige Schrift"; Funk, "New Testament as Tradition and as Canon," 154–64.

uting to the substance and determining the shape of the canon does not suffice to confirm the Catholic principle of tradition or to discredit the Protestant principle of scripture alone, but it does require a reconsideration of both in the light of the actual, historical relationship between scripture and tradition. Among Protestant scholars the normative status of the canon is often defended today precisely through an appeal to tradition. It is argued, for example, that the canon comprises specifically apostolic tradition and that this is distinct from and normative for (later) ecclesiastical tradition both because the apostolic office is incapable of succession and because in shaping the canon the church meant to submit itself permanently to the witness of the apostles.[34] But without subscribing to these particular arguments, the authority of the canon can also be maintained by the claim that it constitutes the original, earliest, or primary tradition of Christianity, and that it has a unique significance because it stands in close spatio-temporal relation to the generative events of Christianity which are otherwise inaccessible.[35] Obviously, such formulations do not concede anything to tradition as a source of authoritative teaching independently of scripture but regard the role of subsequent ecclesiastical tradition as the proper interpretation and exposition of scripture. On the Catholic side, in addition to the remarkable emergence and excellence of critical biblical scholarship in the wake of Vatican II, there are promising reappraisals of the concept of tradition, especially in relation to the decrees of the Council of Trent which have been often interpreted, but probably wrongly, to define tradition as an independent source of revelation.[36] At the same time there is within Protestantism a growing awareness that traditions of teaching and usage which are by no means exclusively biblical also belong to it, and that a radical disavowal of tradition in the name of scripture is historically naive and theologically untenable. Historical studies are making it ever clearer that in the ancient church scripture and tradition were not two separate categories but were mutual and coinherent modes of preserving and proclaiming the faith.[37] Exegesis and the study of the history of the canon only contribute to a fuller appreciation of the organic nature of this relationship.

34. Cullmann, "The Tradition." For telling criticisms, see Lönning, *Kanon im Kanon*, 253–63.

35. See, among others, Ebeling, " 'Sola Scriptura' and Tradition"; Hahn, "Das Problem 'Schrift und Tradition' im Urchristentum," *EvTh* 30 (1970): 449–68.

36. For reappraisal of the Tridentine formulation, see esp. G. Tavard, *Holy Writ or Holy Church? The Crisis of the Protestant Reformation* (New York: Harper & Brothers, 1959), esp. 209.

37. In addition to Tavard, see E. Flesseman van Leer, *Tradition and Scripture in the Early Church* (Assen: Van Gorcum, 1954), and R. P. C. Hanson, *Tradition in the Early Church*.

The transmission of tradition and the missionary expansion of Christianity inevitably gave rise from the beginning to multiple interpretations of the Christian faith. These interpretations necessarily varied according to their cultural and chronological settings, for without such adaptation the Christian message risked the loss of meaning and relevance. But precisely because the settings of Christianity were and continue to be diverse, no single interpretation of Christianity can claim to be conclusive and complete. At the same time, an interpretation which is not rooted in and continuous with the generative events of Christianity will hardly be legitimate. The genius and the value of the NT canon lie in its accommodation of both these factors. The boundaries of the canon rule out certain particular interpretations and some types of interpretation, but the same boundaries encompass a range of other interpretations. Thus, the canon is a compromise between the single and specific ground of faith—the Christ event—and the multiplicity of its interpretive appropriations.[38] It stands against a stultifying self-consistent reduction of meaning, but equally against the vagaries of unlimited possibilities of meaning. In doing so, it makes interpretation both possible and necessary.*

38. Funk, "The New Testament as Tradition and Canon," 174.

*The publication of Brevard Childs' The New Testament as Canon, An Introduction (Philadelphia: Fortress Press, 1984) occurred only after the present study was in proofs, and consequently it could not be taken into account in the foregoing discussion of "The Canon as a Hermeneutical Context" (pp. 73–82 above). Childs' book is the first systematic and extensive effort to apply canonical criticism to the NT. As such it demonstrates in a provocative way both the possibilities and the limitations of making theological exegesis dependent upon the shape of the canon while sharply restricting the significance of historical interpretation. In spite of his disclaimers, it appears to me that Childs has gone much too far in differentiating theological exegesis from historical criticism, and thereby tends to dehistoricize the canon in regard both to the composition of individual documents and to the actual history of the canon. On the other hand, the method of canonical criticism as Childs defines and uses it is impressionistic and tends to yield theological platitudes in the description of the "canonical function" of the documents. Nevertheless, the book is a pioneering effort which is certain to stimulate continuing discussion of the hermeneutical import of the canon.

Appendix: The Full Text of the Muratorian Canon List

. . . at which however he was present and so he has set it down.
The third Gospel book, that according to Luke.
This physician Luke, after Christ's ascension,
since Paul had taken him with him as a companion of his travels,
composed it in his own name
according to his thinking. Yet neither did he himself
see the Lord in the flesh, and thus as he was able to ascertain it,
so he also begins to tell the story from the birth of John.
The fourth of the Gospels, that of John [one] of the disciples.
When his fellow disciples and bishops urged him he
said: "Fast with me from today for three days, and
what will be revealed to each one
let us relate to one another." In the same night it was
revealed to Andrew, [one] of the apostles, that,
while all were to go over [it], John in his own name
should write everything down. And therefore, though
various rudiments are taught in the several
Gospel books, yet that matters
nothing for the faith of believers, since by the one guiding Spirit
everything is declared in all: concerning the birth,
concerning the passion, concerning the resurrection,
concerning the intercourse with his disciples
and concerning his two comings,
the first despised in humility, which has come to pass,
the second glorious in royal power,
which is yet to come. What
wonder then if John so constantly
adduces particular points in his epistles also,

where he says of himself: What we have seen with
our eyes and have heard with our ears and
our hands have handled, these things we have written to you.
For so he professes [himself] not merely an eye and ear witness,
but also a writer of all the marvels of the Lord in order.
The acts of all the apostles, however,
were written in one volume. Luke summarized "for most excellent
  Theophilus"
particular things which happened in his own presence,
as he also clearly indicates by omitting the martyrdom of Peter
as well as the departure of Paul from the city
[of Rome] as he proceeded to Spain. The epistles
of Paul themselves, however, indicate to those who wish to know
which ones [they are], from what place, and for what reason they were
  sent:
first of all, to the Corinthians, admonishing [them] against the schism
of heresy; then to the Galatians, against circumcision;
then to the Romans, however, he wrote at length,
explaining with a series of Scripture quotations
that Christ is their essential principle also. It is necessary
for us to discuss these individually, since the blessed
apostle Paul himself, following the example of his predecessor
John, wrote only to seven churches by name,
and in the following order: the first to the Corinthians,
the second to the Ephesians, the third to the Philippians,
the fourth to the Colossians, the fifth to the Galatians,
the sixth to the Thessalonians, and the seventh
to the Romans. (Although he wrote a second time to the Corinthians
and Thessalonians for reproof, it is evident
that one Church is spread throughout
the whole world. For John also, although
in the Apocalypse he wrote to seven churches,
nevertheless speaks to all.) And one to Philemon
and one to Titus, but two to Timothy, written from affection
and love, have been sanctified by the acknowledgment of the catholic
Church for the ordering of
ecclesiastical discipline. Also current is
[a letter] to the Laodiceans, another to the Alexandrians, forged
in Paul's name for the heresy of Marcion, and several others,
which cannot be accepted in the catholic Church,

for gall cannot be mixed with honey.
Of course the epistle of Jude and
two with the title "John" are accepted in the catholic Church, and Wisdom,
written by friends of Solomon in his honor.
We accept only the apocalypses of John
and Peter, although some of us
do not want it [i.e., Peter] to be read in the Church. But Hermas
composed The Shepherd quite recently in our times in the city
of Rome, while his brother, Pius,
occupied the episcopal seat of the city of Rome. And therefore
it should indeed be read, but
it cannot be read publicly to the people in church either among
the prophets, whose number is complete, nor among
the apostles, for it is after their time.
But we accept nothing whatsoever of Arsinoes, or Valentinus,
or Miltiades. Those also [are rejected] who
composed a new book of psalms for Marcion,
together with Basilides, the founder of the
Cataphrygians of Asia Minor.

Manufactured by Amazon.ca
Bolton, ON